Friends & Friendship

The Secrets of Drawing Closer

Jerry and Mary White

NAVPRESS
A MINISTRY OF THE NAVIGATORS
P.O. Box 6000, Colorado Springs, Colorado 80934

The Navigators is an international,
evangelical Christian organization.
Jesus Christ gave his followers the Great
Commission to go and make disciples
(Matthew 28:19). The aim of The
Navigators is to help fulfill that commis-
sion by multiplying laborers for Christ in
every nation.

NavPress is the publishing ministry of
The Navigators. NavPress publications
are tools to help Christians grow.
Although publications alone cannot
make disciples or change lives, they can
help believers learn biblical discipleship,
and apply what they learn to their lives
and ministries.

Third printing, 1983

Printed in the United States of America

Contents

Contents

Authors

Jerry White is the Pacific Regional Director for The Navigators in the United States. He holds a Ph.D. in astronautics. During thirteen years with the United States Air Force, he served as a space mission controller at Cape Canaveral and taught for six years at the U.S. Air Force Academy. He is now a lieutenant colonel in the U.S. Air Force Reserve.

Mary Ann Knutson White attended Northwestern Bible College and the University of Washington. She holds a degree in English from the University of Colorado, and has worked as a secretary in government and private industry.

The Whites' first contact with The Navigators was at the University of Washington. They later helped begin

Navigator ministries at the Air Force Academy and Purdue University, and are currently involved in discipling ministries, speaking at seminars, and ministering in their local church.

Jerry and Mary live near Seattle and have four children: Stephen, Katherine, Karen, and Kristin.

OTHER BOOKS
by Jerry and Mary White
    Your Job: Survival or Satisfaction?
    The Christian in Mid-life
by Mary White
    Successful Family Devotions
by Jerry White
    Honesty, Morality, and Conscience
    The Christian Student's How-To-Study Guide

To
Robert and Frances McCarthy,
Roger and Joanne Brandt,
and Chris and Alice Canlis—
three "generations" of friends
who have
loved us and influenced us.
Their stimulating friendships
have enriched our lives
and given us the ideals
that form the foundation
of this book.

CHAPTER 1
The Ideal Friend

A winter's day
in a deep and dark December:
I am alone,
gazing from my window
to the streets below
on a freshly fallen, silent shroud of snow.
*   I am a rock,*
*   I am an island.*

I've built walls,
a fortress deep and mighty,
that none may penetrate.
I have no need of friendship;
friendship causes pain.

It's laughter and it's loving I disdain.
  I am a rock,
  I am an island.

Don't talk of love;
well, I've heard the word before;
it's sleeping in my memory.
I won't disturb the slumber
of feelings that have died.
If I never loved
I never would have cried.
  I am a rock,
  I am an island.

I have my books
and my poetry to protect me;
I am shielded in my armor,
hiding in my room, safe within my womb.
I touch no one
and no one touches me.
  I am a rock,
  I am an island.

And a rock feels no pain;
and an island never cries.
                              —Paul Simon

LONELINESS...PAIN...CRYING...all are vestiges of broken friendships. Yet no one can have a meaningful existence without love and friendship. They are the substance of our emotional life. We seek them constantly, but they often elude our grasp or else disappoint us. Sometimes we offer them to others only to have them rejected.

We desperately need and want deep relationships, but all too often we find it difficult to develop that ideal friendship. We all experience brief tastes of deepening friendship, and know more is possible, yet the process of actually developing and deepening those friendships is frustrated by lack of time or mutual interest. When they do develop, we puzzle over how to maintain them, and how to overcome the discord which inevitably occurs in regular interaction.

One of the greatest pleasures of our lives has been our number of deep friendships which continue to this day. These friends have encouraged and confronted us. They have been the ones we called in time of need and in time of joy.

But not everyone enjoys friendships like these, and most of us have gone through troubling times when friends seemed scarce. Many people are lonely. Many are insulated from in-depth interaction of any kind, either by choice or by exclusion.

We wish we could say that Christians don't experience this frustration in friendship. But we can't. People are lonely in the church as well as in the world. Christians do have a different basis, however, on which to build friendships. Although the principles are the same for both, their application—in the motivations and in the frustrations of friendship—is significantly different.

That is what this book is all about—the whys and hows of Christian friendship.

Defining Friendship

Defining a friend is like trying to define beauty: It's often in the eye of the beholder. Each person has a personal standard which he may not even be able to articulate.

But as difficult as definition may be, we must attempt to define it in order to talk about it. In a study we developed to aid in this task, we took written surveys of more than three hundred married and single men and women, ranging in age from eighteen to eighty-two. Each person was asked to write "a brief definition of a friend." Here are some characteristic replies:

"Someone you can bare your soul to and not be afraid it will get around. Someone who will tell you when your slip is showing. Someone who shares loving concern and tactful truth" (woman, age thirty-one).

"One who knows you well and loves you anyway" (woman, age sixty-six).

"Loyal in hard times, fun to be with, and have common interests" (man, age twenty-six).

"A person who understands you, appreciates your views, loyal. A person who has quite a few common interests with you" (man, age fifty-two).

"Someone to share experiences with" (man, age fifty-five).

"Someone who enjoys being around you, accepts you for who you are, and is faithful to you when the chips are down" (man, age twenty-four).

"One who I can share my heart with no matter what is on it and still be accepted for who I am, and vice versa. One who I can be honest with for good or bad. One who I love being with and sharing things with. One who is a good listener" (woman, age twenty-nine).

"A friend is someone in whom you have unlimited trust; they will share with you deeply and honestly. The things shared between you go beyond opinions and observations" (woman, under thirty).

"One whom I can share my deepest thoughts, desires, and feelings with in confidence. Available twenty-four hours a day and a faithful prayer warrior" (man, age twenty-nine).

"Someone who knows me intimately and is committed to my best under all circumstances regardless of the risks to our relationship" (man, age thirty-one).

"A person I enjoy spending time with and can share my feelings, thoughts and experiences with. The best friends listen and accept me, but will also confront me so I can grow" (woman, age twenty-two).

"Someone you can relate to and trust with what you share" (man, age twenty-three).

Each of these definitions is a subjective *perception* of friendship, and not necessarily an accurate reflection of reality. Your definition of friendship might not look anything like the ones we listed here, since your individual experience is different from everyone else's. But certain phrases or words which appear repeatedly in the responses above reveal what most people *want* in a friendship: loyalty, sharing deeply, keeping confidences, friendship in spite of faults, mutual interests, and common activities.

We can each imagine the ideal friend, but we rarely find one who is perfect. All of us have faults. So how do we arrive at a realistic definition of a friend? Consider this definition, which focuses on the crucial ingredients of any Christian friendship:

> A friend is a trusted confidant to whom I am mutually drawn as a companion and an ally, whose love for me is not dependent on my performance, and whose influence draws me closer to God.

Characteristics of the Ideal Friend

An exhaustive list describing the many nuances of friendship would fill many pages—perhaps many books!

And after listing them, who could really fulfill them?

We identified eight prominent characteristics of a good friend, based upon our own research and what we discovered in the Scriptures. Remember that no one can match them all perfectly. One of our own children frequently comments, "Well, no one is perfect!" Do the best you can to live up to them, and use them to help you gauge your friendship performance. (On page 183 of this book is a Self-Evaluation Inventory which can help you determine your own strengths as a personal friend and point out weak areas which may need extra effort.)

Loyal. We all want friends who are loyal to us, friends we can trust and rely on. No one wants a fair weather friend who disappears at the first sign of trouble or personal inconvenience. Proverbs 19:4-7 speaks clearly about the transitory nature of friendship based only on wealth, position, or power.

> Wealth brings many friends,
>> but a poor man's friend deserts him.
> Many curry favor with a ruler,
>> and everyone is the friend of a man who gives gifts.
> A poor man is shunned by all his relatives—
>> how much more do his friends avoid him!
> Though he pursues them with pleading,
>> they are nowhere to be found.

"He pursues them with pleading." What a sad but accurate picture of one whose friends were disloyal. The tendency to be disloyal resides in each one of us.

Ann was desperate to share her burden with someone. She was a new member in her church and had no close friends there. But she was impressed with Liz, who seemed friendly and open with her and who had made special efforts to spend time with her at various social functions. Ann decided to take the risk and call her.

"Hello, Liz? This is Ann—Ann Carlson. I know this might be an imposition on you, but I just have to talk to someone. Would you have time to talk this evening?"

Liz was very accommodating. They met and Ann shared deeply from her life, particularly about how she had just lost her job because she was unable to work under the pressure of a particular department. She said she felt like she was about to have a nervous breakdown.

Liz listened very attentively and offered a few suggestions of sound advice. Then they prayed together.

A week later, after the morning service, a woman Ann had seen a couple of times came up to her.

"Ann, here is a book I thought might interest you."

Ann looked at the title: *The Christian and Emotional Health*. She cringed inside. Did this woman know something? She thanked her and took the book. A few minutes later, one of the leaders in the church came by and said, "Hi, Ann. Just want you to know we are praying for you."

Ann began to get furious inside. Had Liz said something? Later she found Liz had shared "a confidential prayer request for Ann" in a small prayer group. Ann was hurt and angry. Soon she left the church without ever developing a friendship with Liz.

Few things destroy a friendship more quickly than a broken confidence. "A brother offended is harder to be won than a strong city" (Proverbs 18:19, *New American Standard Bible*). The Scriptures teach that true loyalty is not common. "Many a man proclaims his own loyalty, but who can find a trustworthy man?" (Proverbs 20:6, NASB).

A mainstay of loyalty is *unbroken confidences*. We must not violate what others tell us. Open sharing needs the security of private communication.

In some cases the confidences should not even be shared with a spouse. Some couple-to-couple friendships assume that what is shared with one partner will be told to the other. Make certain this is the case before discussing a friend's situation with your spouse.

Serious issues, however—like threats of suicide, deep psychological problems, or dangers to others—pose a unique problem. We bear a responsibility in these cases to obtain competent professional help. But these are unusual in the kinds of friendships we're concerned with, so as a general rule follow these principles:

> If you argue your case with a neighbor,
>> do not betray another man's confidence,
> or he who hears it may shame you
>> and you will never lose your bad reputation.
>>>> (Proverbs 25:9–10)
> If you love someone you will be loyal to him
> no matter what the cost. (1 Corinthians 13:7,
> *Living Bible*)

Loyalty means *defending your friend.* When someone criticizes or gossips about your friend, what do you do? One of the loneliest remarks the apostle Paul made is found in 2 Timothy 4:16. "At my first defense, no one came to my support, but everyone deserted me." We all need a spokesman and defender—not one who abandons the truth in our defense, but one who speaks the truth in love.

Loyalty also means *supporting a friend in difficulty as well as prosperity.* "A friend loves at all times, and a brother is born for adversity" (Proverbs 17:17). We need friends desperately in times of problems and difficulty. One friend of ours said that when he was going through deep spiritual turmoil for over fifteen years, all but two of his friends virtually deserted him. Adversity reveals the depth of friendship. And adversity is not just those catastrophic happenings of life and death when many rally around, but also those deep waters that only a few know we are passing through. Friendship really deepens when we pass through those difficulties together.

Shares deeply. The overwhelming consensus in our survey of values in friendship was that "sharing deeply" is a very important characteristic of friendship. Just under half of the respondents listed it as their most important quality in friendship, and most ranked it as one of their top three.

But what does it mean to share deeply? Each individual has his own understanding of what constitutes deep sharing. To some it means revealing our innermost thoughts, feelings, and fears. As one woman said, "The conversations can be made up of statements about personal feelings that you aren't sure of and need reassurance about, even if they sound totally nonsensical." To others, it is primarily mental—the sharing of philosophical issues. To still others it is venting anger and feelings and frustrations not normally accepted in public.

True open sharing does not spring up overnight. It must be developed through time and experience. Although each individual reveals his inner self in various degrees according to his personality and background, certain fundamentals of the sharing process are common. These are listening, speaking, accepting, and understanding— the four key ingredients of intimate and honest communication.

1. *Listening* is essential to communication between friends. "My dear brothers, take note of this: Everyone should be quick to listen, slow to speak and slow to become angry" (James 1:19).

What does it mean to be "quick to listen"? Do we listen

faster, like turning a 33⅓-rpm record up to 78-rpm? No. We open our ears and alert our minds to both words *and* meaning. We listen instead of talk. It's been said, "God gave us two ears and one mouth, so we can listen twice as much as we talk." That's good advice.

Listening is hard work. It takes concentration and patience. Too often we listen only enough to figure out when our turn will come to talk. Our nervous "Uh-huhs" and shifting eyes reveal our impatience. We've all experienced this disinterest from someone "listening" to us, and can painfully recall the sense of rejection we felt. Yet we do it to others.

We need to listen to *what is said* (the words), the *message conveyed* (the ideas or thought), its *meaning* (what is behind the ideas or thoughts), and the *message behind the words* (listening between the lines).

2. *Speaking* is important too, but it should be done in moderation, with thought and concern. "He who answers before listening—that is his folly and his shame" (Proverbs 18:13). Proverbs 25:11 tells us that "a word aptly spoken is like apples of gold in settings of silver."

Our friends do want to know what we think of their sharing, but we need to respond wisely. Even if the friendship is very strong, we still are not free to say just anything. We bear a heavy responsibility for how we speak—"The tongue that brings healing is a tree of life, but a deceitful tongue crushes the spirit" (Proverbs 15:4). We need to be both wise and honest in what we say.

Don't be afraid to speak, but don't be afraid of silence, either. We don't need a constant flow of chatter to make someone feel like a friend. Sometimes we don't hear our friends because we are speaking too much. In the silence perhaps you can both think more clearly. There is a time for speaking and a time for listening. Wisdom is knowing when to do which. "Do not let any unwholesome talk come out of your mouths, but only what is helpful for building others up according to their needs, that it may benefit those who listen" (Ephesians 4:29).

In the beginning of my long-standing friendship with Joanne, I felt the conversations were sometimes strained. Joanne was a quiet person and I felt I needed to keep a conversation going. Finally I realized that I was talking too much and was not getting to know what Joanne felt or thought. So I resolved to cut back on my talking and wait for Joanne to speak, even if it meant times of silence. As I did this, there were some silences—at first. But soon Joanne began sharing more, and I found that if I had kept quiet earlier in our relationship, I would have discovered what an interesting person my new friend was.—(Mary)

3. Fostering deep sharing requires large doses of accepting the other person. In our survey, many people emphasized the importance of being accepted just as they were. We communicate lack of acceptance with our eyes, our posture, our facial expressions, and our tone of voice. Do you remember the last time you spoke to someone who made you feel like you had bad breath? It's such an uncomfortable feeling that we want to get away as quickly as possible.

Acceptance is not approval, nor is it agreement with everything a person does or says. Jesus accepted us totally while disapproving of our sin. Our response should communicate, "I accept you totally for who you are, though I may not always agree with what you say or do." Acceptance means we can put our arm around someone and say, "Tom, I don't think I agree with what you just said, but let's discuss it. I may have misunderstood."

Sometimes we communicate acceptance by our lack of response to a baited question, or by our lack of shock at a supposedly shocking statement. If we don't extend this acceptance we slam the door on intimate sharing.

4. Speaking and accepting will fail, however, without a root of *understanding*. Hearing the words and even the message are not sufficient. The message must be understood. It has been said that "Loneliness is not in being alone, for then ministering spirits come to soothe and bless—loneliness is to endure the presence of one who does not understand."

I have heard my children speak but had my attention focused on something else.

"Dad, you're not listening."

"Yes, I am. I can repeat what you just said." And I proceed to do so.

"But Dad, you're not really listening."

And they're right. I heard the words but didn't listen with attention and understanding. But the most difficult interaction with my children takes place when they say, "Dad, you really wouldn't understand." And no amount of discussion can convince them otherwise. Somehow I communicated a lack of understanding.

True understanding is a gift from God. "For the Lord gives wisdom, and from his mouth come knowledge and understanding" (Proverbs 2:6). The understanding referred to here is of God. God can give us clear understanding of other people through our knowledge of him. "The fear of the Lord is the beginning of wisdom, and knowledge of the Holy One is understanding" (Proverbs 9:10).

If you have a godly concern for your friends you will receive insight from God. We need this insight to be a true friend. We may not be able to share every feeling and hurt that friends have, but we can accept them and try to understand. This forms a foundation for a strong, sharing friendship.

Fun to be with. Although having fun is somewhat lighter than the two weighty characteristics of loyalty and deep sharing, it is important. Deep friends do not sit around all day defending one another, sharing deep emotional feelings, and engaging in philosophical discourse. They have fun together. They laugh, kid, and enjoy doing things together. What a dreary relationship it would be if fun were not a part of the friendship!

Do you have friends who will call on the spur of the moment and say, "Come on over and go to the park with us for a picnic lunch"? Not only are you not upset because they didn't give you two days notice, but you drop everything and go—and have a great time. You enjoy being with them. We rarely consider the requests of good friends an imposition on our time. And they don't get offended if we can't respond to their invitations.

As you develop a friendship, look for common interests—tennis, reading, sewing, hiking, decorating, cars, gardening. Think of creative things to do together—plays, sports, a baseball game, a spontaneous birthday party, a picnic at the lake, a two-day vacation with another family, or a surprise work party to help a friend with garden work.

Recently a friend in our Bible study suggested that we go to a Seattle Mariners' baseball game together. I had never gone to a major league game, nor had Jerry. Jerry looked forward to it, yet I thought it would be boring just sitting for three hours watching what I assumed would be a slow-moving game. Yet I wanted

*to be with our friends, so I agreed to go. Much to my
surprise, I had a wonderful time. We had lots of
conversation between pitches. We switched seats
several times to talk with someone else. And we got
into the spirit of the game by standing up occasionally
and cheering the Mariners. There was far more action
to watch than I had anticipated, plus we had the
enjoyment of being with our friends in an informal
atmosphere.*

Enjoyment should be natural and mutual. Do you
initiate fun activities? You don't have to take turns
providing a fun atmosphere. Allow these things to happen
spontaneously. Enjoy your friends. Keep some vitality in
the relationship by having fun together and sharing
experiences.

Stimulating. Each individual is unique. Because we
are not alike, we stimulate each other mentally and
emotionally. "As iron sharpens iron, so one man sharpens
another" (Proverbs 27:17). A friend should stimulate us to
new ways of thinking, to personal growth, and to spiritual
development. Have you ever noticed that some relationships drag you down and depress you?

We should stimulate others to their best in life, so they
can look back and say that they were enriched by our
friendship, rather than bored and mentally dried up by it.

Often, such a vitalizing friendship begins out of some
practical or particular need such as a problem, a mutual
interest, or a common objective or activity. To continue a
relationship, it then must grow through mutual stimulation. Consequently, people of similar intellectual ability,
social status, or employment often develop friendships.

*I always enjoy being with my dear friend Jean
Fleming. She regularly challenges me with new*

insights. I love the way her mind works. Her book, A Mother's Heart (NavPress, 1982), is just a glimpse of the creative way she seeks to stimulate her children to grow as people and to know God. After spending a few hours with her, I always have some new thought about the Lord, or about life in general. Yet she is not a somber person, but fun-loving and witty. Jean typifies the type of stimulating friend everyone should have. —(Mary)

Remember that stimulation is only a part of friendship and should not be overemphasized. And it is not something that can be forced. We shouldn't force ourselves on our friends, but instead just be ourselves and offer that part of us that can attract and enliven their own lives.

It's possible to try too hard to be stimulating. One friend may feel strongly that he must constantly share new ideas and challenge old ways of thinking, until the friendship loses its spontaneity and relaxed atmosphere. Another may continually challenge his friend about the validity of what he says. Within these extremes lies the potential of helping our friends live fuller lives. "Let us consider how to stimulate one another to love and good deeds" (Hebrews 10:24, NASB).

If this sounds vague to you or makes you think you have to be an intellectual giant in order to be a good friend, here are some practical suggestions:

- Help your friend solve a practical problem in his home if you are handy with repairs. Show him how as you do it with him.
- Ask nonthreatening questions about decisions and plans. "How does that model car rate for maintenance and repairs?" "Will your vacation include stops at some of the national parks or monuments

in that area?" "I just read a book that I think you will like. Would you like to take a look at it?"

● Share alternate ideas for problems they may be facing. "Have you considered letting your teenagers budget a fixed amount of the family money for all of their expenses?"

● Share a new experience.

● Ask for their counsel or help.

● Propose some new activity to do together (such as a class at the community college, a seminar on child raising, a concert, or a sightseeing drive or hike).

Encouraging. Have you ever spent time with a person and gone away depressed? A friendship that regularly drags you down cannot survive. We need to be encouraged, and to encourage others, even in the midst of fun, laughter, and play. Encouragement provides increased self-esteem, a brighter outlook on life, more positive thinking, and spiritual uplifting.

We can build up our friends and give them hope by our attitudes and our words. We do it by sharing Scripture or praying together, and by lifting their loads in times of pressure. We have been encouraged when friends have called to tell us they were praying for us, or volunteered to take care of our children during a crisis, to run errands for us, or to listen when we need to talk.

Encouragement comes in little ways—words, a note, a flower, a gift, a listening ear. It is confirmed by our presence. We encourage by being loyal, by sharing and allowing others to share deeply, by having fun, and by stimulating our friends.

Encouraging others can keep them from sin. "But encourage one another daily, as long as it is called Today, so that none of you may be hardened by sin's deceitfulness" (Hebrews 3:13). The result of our encouraging can be much more than just making our friends feel good.

Self-sacrificing. "Greater love has no one than this, that one lay down his life for his friends" (John 15:13). A true friend gives sacrificially to meet the pressing needs of another person. Though we may not be asked to give up our lives for our friends, we will expend energy, time, and personal resources to help them. We should give of ourselves regardless of the cost to us.

A striking biblical example of sacrificial friendship is that of David and Jonathan. As Saul's son, Jonathan was the rightful heir to the throne of Israel. He knew David would be king one day, but he sacrificed his own future by protecting and defending his friend David. He gave up his own chance for the kingdom out of his love for David.

The test of sacrificial friendship is our response to a call for help. Would you...

- set aside personal interest to help?
- cancel a vacation to meet a pressing need?
- give money to help even though you have little money yourself?
- spend exhausting time in prayer?
- accept others' children temporarily or even permanently?

Self-sacrifice instead of selfishness is the measure of our depth of friendship. "Each of you should look not only to your own interests, but also to the interests of others" (Philippians 2:4).

Loving. The *agape* love of the Greek New Testament must undergird our friendship. This love is self-sacrificing, expecting nothing in return.

But assuming we really do love our friends, how do we demonstrate this love? We certainly express love by our actions toward our friends; but we also need to say the simple words "I love you." For some (especially men to other men) this is awkward. In praying together you might say, "Lord, thanks for Jack. I value his friendship and love him very much." And let's not be afraid of a warm embrace. Not the awkward, perfunctory embrace that replaces a cold handshake, but a true expression of friendship, as some might demonstrate in a warm two-handed handshake.

Few people have problems with some affection toward a friend of the same sex, but many are cautious about physical demonstration of affection for the opposite sex. We so often associate sexual overtones to such action. Certainly, discretion is appropriate, but let's not be so rigid that touch or embrace is absolutely forbidden.

As I traveled overseas a few years ago I met a woman missionary friend. Since I was just passing through her city we spent only an hour or two in the airport. I asked her if there was anything I could do to help her, as she had been going through some difficult circumstances. After a moment's thought, she said, "I think I just need a hug."—(Jerry)

Ask God to give you an honest love for your friends.

Spiritually challenging. Dan was a man who developed deep friendships and valued them greatly. He was loyal and stimulating. When these friends were Christians the effect in his life was positive. Later, his circle of friends became almost entirely non-Christian. Slowly, they drew him away from God. Soon he took on their lifestyle and beliefs. He now has isolated himself from Christian influence and has virtually no walk with God.

Friends drive you to or from God. Therefore it is vital that many of your friends share a strong view of the

Christian life. God must be a part of your friendship — both in what you do and in what you talk about. As a friend, do you stimulate others to a closer walk with God? Do you converse easily on spiritual issues? Do you pray together? Do you share common spiritual concerns? The principle of Proverbs 13:20 applies here. "He who walks with the wise grows wise, but a companion of fools suffers harm." We also read in 1 Corinthians 15:33, "Do not be misled: 'Bad company corrupts good character.'"

Our friendships deeply influence our spiritual life. Does this mean that we eliminate new friendships with non-Christians? Certainly not. Such friendships are essential. But it does mean that our primary friendships must have a strong spiritual dimension.

A friend is characterized, then, by the eight important qualities shown in Figure 1-1.

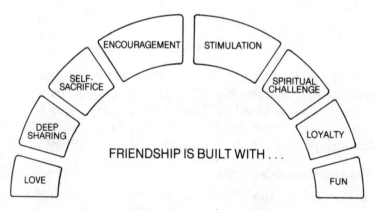

Figure 1-1: The primary characteristics of a friend.

These stones, of course, cannot stay suspended in mid-air. What is it that keeps them from falling and supports these characteristics in the building of friendship? The answer is *time* and *effort* (see Figure 1-2 on page 28).

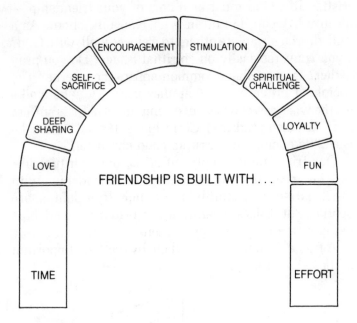

Figure 1-2: Time and Effort support friendship building.

The characteristics of a friend do not appear out of nothing in a relationship. They take time—months and often years—to develop. They take personal effort to build. The remaining chapters will help you build friendships that are characterized by these qualities.

The Ultimate Relationship

As you read the title of this section you probably thought, "Here is the section on marriage." But there is a much more fundamental relationship than marriage. It is our relationship with God.

Up to this point we have assumed that you view friendship from a Christian perspective. But you may not. Certainly deep friendships develop without Christian contexts, just as there are good marriages outside of Christian contexts. But a relationship with God gives a new and deeper meaning to friendship. It provides Jesus Christ as our role model, and he gives us instructions on our relationships and on our motivation for friendship. A non-Christian simply does not have the same foundational resources. Therefore,

> Christians have a different basis than non-Christians
> for building friendships, because their role model
> is Jesus Christ and they have his resources to draw on.

In our search for fulfilling friendships, then, we should apply this principle:

> The first and most fundamental friendship
> of life is with Jesus Christ.

Two levels of this friendship are relevant at this point. The first is initially entering into a relationship with Jesus Christ—the birth of the relationship. The second is developing into a committed disciple of Jesus Christ—the growth of the relationship.

A person enters a relationship with God by a simple realization that our sin has separated us from God and we need to be forgiven. Jesus Christ was the Son of God, and lived a perfect, sinless life on earth. He died in our place for our sin, and then he rose from the dead. He offers us a permanent, eternal relationship with God by simply believing in him for our personal salvation.

His self-sacrificing act is declared in 1 Corinthians 15:3-4: "For what I received I passed on to you as of first importance: that Christ died for our sins according to the Scriptures, that he was buried, that he was raised on the third day according to the Scriptures."

A simple prayer confessing your need for Christ and

your faith in him gives you birth as a Christian. To experience the true depth of Christian friendship, you need this personal relationship with Christ.

So for a Christian to lay the continuing foundation of friendship he must have daily personal communication with Christ himself.

> When a person's foundational relationship with Jesus
> Christ is fulfilling and satisfying, his friendships
> with others will begin to fall into place.

Now we can see that the arch in Figure 1-2 is still incomplete. It needs the fundamental relationship in Jesus Christ as a foundation.

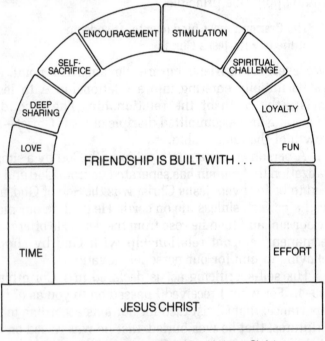

Figure 1-3: A personal relationship with Jesus Christ forms the foundation for friendship.

"So then, just as you received Christ Jesus as Lord, continue to live in him, *rooted and built up* in him, strengthened in the faith as you were taught, and overflowing with thankfulness" (Colossians 2:6-7).

Summary

1. A friend is a trusted confidant to whom I am mutually drawn as a companion and ally, whose love for me is not dependent on my performance, and whose influence draws me closer to God.

2. A friend is primarily:
    loyal, one who shares deeply, fun, stimulating, encouraging, self-sacrificing, loving, and spiritually challenging.

These qualities are undergirded by time and effort and built on the foundation of Jesus Christ.

Principles

1. Christians have a different basis than non-Christians for building friendships, because their role model is Jesus Christ and they have his resources to draw on.

2. The first and most fundamental friendship of life is with Jesus Christ.

3. When a person's foundational relationship with Jesus Christ is fulfilling and satisfying, his friendships with others will begin to fall into place.

CHAPTER 2
The Realities of Friendship

Y OU SAW A picture of the ideal friend in chapter one
and may have found yourself lacking in several
areas. If you've worked through the Self-Evaluation
Inventory and didn't get a perfect score, you may be
wondering if you can *ever* achieve a model friendship.
Don't close the book! Good news is coming.

First, you're with the majority of us in not being a
perfect friend. Second, no one can maintain all of his
friendships at that ideal level. Third, it's not hard to grow
significantly in a *few* of your friendships.

To help you understand the variations in friendship,
think of all the people you would include in some category
as friends. To some you would give your last dollar. With
others you only drink coffee at the office. Some are

neighbors whom you talk with a few times a week and others you see regularly at church. Some you play sports with and others you talk to when you have particular needs. Co-workers, relatives, partners, church members, Sunday school teachers, bosses, buddies, neighbors, high school classmates, former teachers, pastors, and a host of others make up the collage of your friendship circle. Or is it just an acquaintance circle? Let's divide this multitude of "friends" into meaningful groups.

Acquaintances

Author Rollo May has suggested that most people make five hundred to twenty-five hundred acquaintances each year, but have fewer than seven personal friends. Most of us make a large number of *acquaintances* in such contexts as shopping, working, and church whom we never intend to pursue as friends. We usually accept these people as simply passing through transient relationships with us in the normal course of daily living.

Level One: Casual Friends

Out of this fishing pool of acquaintances emerge a number of people whom we begin to draw into another type of relationship. We can call this first level of friendship *casual friends*.

This group consists of people we see *regularly* in the normal course of living. We know them by their first names and occasionally initiate social contacts with them. They include church friends, some co-workers, neighbors, club associates, former classmates, and many others. They may number from twenty to a hundred or more, depending upon the breadth of our social contacts and our aggressiveness in getting to know people. These friends may last for a few months or a lifetime. The more we move and meet new acquaintances the more people we include in this list. The casual friends category may also include a number of relatives with whom we maintain only limited contact.

We can picture this friendship category culled from the general pool of our acquaintances, and serving as a broad base for more selective friendships (Figure 2-1).

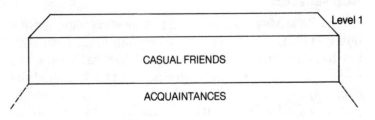

Figure 2-1: Levels of friendship.

Though casual friends are important to the social and economic matrix of our relationships in a local society, they rarely satisfy our personal hunger for close and meaningful friendship. A person can be lonely in a crowd of casual friends. We want and need more from our relationships with others.

Level Two: Close Friends

We thus move to a second level of friendship which we can generally refer to as *close friends*. Several divisions appear within this group.

We develop a number of close friendships through our various associations, and we can simply refer to these as *associate friendships*. These include co-workers with whom we have a necessarily close working relationship on the job, whether it's with a boss, a subordinate, or an employee.

Neighbors provide another area of association. We've lived in a number of cities over the years and have developed friendships that were close for a period of time. Some continued for many years, and others disappeared a year or two after we moved.

Associate friendships also develop while serving in the church. Our relationships with people on a committee, in a class, with the pastoral staff, or in a counseling situation often develop to the level of closeness. In certain organizations or environments (Christian service groups, Bible study groups, political committees, clubs, and so forth), we often strike up acquaintances which become first casual, then close friends.

Another associate friendship occurs by birth or marriage—relatives. Relationships with relatives vary with proximity and mutual interests.

Many of these friendships may grow in the context of an activity or a common goal such as a neighborhood organization, a small group Bible study, or a team project. Many, if not most, of them recede to the level of casual friendship when the goal, committee, or job is removed.

In addition to close friendships with our associates, we each have friends that we see or talk to frequently who fit the category of *close personal friends*. These people tend to remain close for many years regardless of age and distance. We continue a regular relationship with them by mutual choice.

A final division in Level Two close friendships is that of *mentor*. This is a person who contributes significantly to your life in a teaching or guiding way. It could be the one who counseled you in hard times or who discipled you.

Two of our dear personal friends are our pastor of eighteen years ago, Robert McCarthy, and his wife Frances. For two years they filled a mentor role for us which developed into a permanent, close personal friendship. Others in close association with The Navigators influenced us deeply through the years as mentor friends in discipleship and personal training.

Whether you have a mentor or are a mentor, keep in mind that this kind of relationship is a strong potential source of close friendship. Now let's add this category of close friends to our diagram (see Figure 2-2). The number of friends in this level may range from ten to thirty *active* relationships. Another thirty or so can be *inactive* due to distance. The initial close friendships still remain and revive with little effort when opportunity arises.

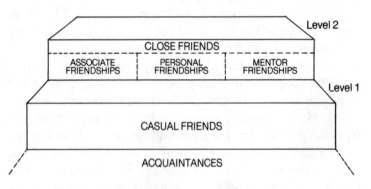

Figure 2-2: Levels of friendship.

We can summarize Level Two close friendships like this:
  1. Associate: Co-workers, people from church, members of organizations, neighbors, relatives.
  2. Personal: Maintained apart from particular circumstances.
  3. Mentor: Leader, teacher, discipler.

Level Three: Intimate (Best) Friends

Even in the category of close friends, however, there are always a few whom we'll want to draw into the inner circle of our lives. This is the level on which the ideal friend of chapter one operates. We can designate this *intimate* or *best* friends.

These friends are the few people to whom we pour out our souls, sharing our deepest feelings and hopes. They meet us at our point of deepest need, and we enjoy and look forward to being with them above all others. These friendships have a lasting quality which develops over months and years.

Obviously, we cannot maintain many Level Three relationships. The respondents to our survey had an average of four current and active intimate friends each; some had only one and others had as many as six.

Level Three completes our diagram (Figure 2-3):

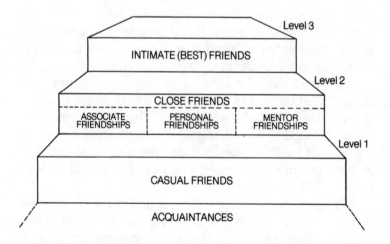

Figure 2-3: Levels of friendship.

The diagram is not intended to separate friend from friend, so don't start making a list of all your friends to pigeonhole them into their respective levels. Instead, use it to help you see the process of friendship development and to form realistic friendship expectations.

Remember that as in all attempts to describe human activity, character, and relationships, no system is precise. These levels overlap and blend as a friendship develops; they're not on-off switches that make a person either one or the other. Your friendship may shift with time and experience.

Friendship Variations

Friendships grow, change, decrease, and get stale. No friendship remains constant. Have you ever attended a ten-year or even a twenty-five-year reunion? What a shock! Not only don't you recognize everyone, but suddenly those old friends are strangers. They've changed. You've changed. Jobs, successes, failures, education, children, and divorces have intersected with their lives as well as yours. If you became a Christian later in life, your entire value system has changed, forming a new basis for friendships.

We must allow for an ebb and flow of our friendships. If we try to force their growth, we'll end up smothering them instead. Part of the beauty of a friendship lies in its freedom to grow and change. Friendship does not grow naturally if we force ourselves on others. "Seldom set foot in your neighbor's house—too much of you, and he will hate you" (Proverbs 25:17).

Friendships constantly flow in and out of Levels One to Three. They vary in time and intensity. Our experience indicates that about two years is minimum for a deep friendship to develop naturally, although some intimate friendships do blossom quickly.

As we consider the variations in friendship, we can state two general principles:

1. Close and intimate friendships take time to develop.
2. Friendships will ebb and flow in intensity over time.

Individual Capacities

We've already stated that we can't be intimate friends with everyone. But the fact is that we can't even be *casual* friends with everyone. As simple as this fact may be, it causes much frustration in the pursuit of deep friendships. You may wish, for instance, to pursue a close or intimate friendship with another person only to find that he's up to capacity in these friendships. As much as he'd like to develop such a friendship with you, he just doesn't have the time unless he eliminates a friendship or at least changes levels with another friend. Most likely, you've also had to turn down someone's friendship initiative because you already had as many close friends as you could handle.

One of our greatest frustrations in the last two years has been our desire for deeper friendships with at least six couples with whom we have done Bible study. We have succeeded with only one couple. We just did not have the time to go beyond the close friendship level with the others, although we did enjoy many of the ideal characteristics in chapter one with more than one couple.

Everyone has a limited capacity for friendship, but that capacity differs with each individual in the number of relationships he or she can sustain or emotionally tolerate.

I have a high capacity for relationships and delight in making new ones. Throughout our marriage this became a point of frustration for Mary and of conflict between us. She would joke that I knew someone in every town we drove through, and our Air Force moves across the country took us through a lot of towns. Then we discovered that I am willing to live with more relationships at a less deep level.

A standing joke, communicated now by a knowing glance, is my frequent conversational references to my "good" friends. "Yes, I know George. He's a good friend of mine." So often my "good" friend is one whom I met at a conference, ate dinner with, and had one long-distance phone conversation with. As we worked on this book, we found our definitions for a "good" friend differed and had to change.

In spite of our definition disparity, we both realized I did possess the capacity to maintain a higher than normal number of close (Level Two) friends. But Mary and I have about the same capacity for intimate (Level Three) relationships.

We can state another general principle, then, about friendship variations from person to person:

> Everyone has a *limited* capacity for friendship,
> and each person has a *different* capacity
> for numbers of friendships.

These capacities are neither good nor bad; they reflect the way God made our personality and emotions. There is no special virtue in maintaining a large number of friends. The key is to live within your capacity and develop to the fullest those friendships that God gives you.

We do believe, however, that your capacity for intimate friendships may actually expand somewhat as you apply the principles taught in this book. Part of that expansion will come from not trying to make every friendship a Level Three relationship or forcing it through an absolutely ideal pattern. As we relax our frustrations, we will enjoy our friendships more and see them deepen.

Assess your capacity for intimate friends. If it is two or three, be content. But if you have no friends at the intimate level, ask God to fill that void to capacity. You need this kind of friend. "Two are better than one, because they have a good return for their work: If one falls down, his friend can help him up. But pity the man who falls and has no one to help him up!" (Ecclesiastes 4:9-10).

In addition to their difference in capacity, people also differ in their inherent ability to pursue deep friendship. One who is shy, or who comes from a home where feelings were seldom expressed, or who has an abrasive person-ality, may find it especially difficult to deepen rela-tionships. But he can still do it, with time and effort.

We may envy those who seem to attract people like magnets and whose conversations flow with ease. But don't waste energy in envy, for many of these people live with a multitude of only surface or casual friendships, and long for close and intimate relationships where the harder issues of loyalty, love, and spiritual challenge undergird the friendship. Keep this principle in mind when you're pursuing friendships:

> Every person has the capacity to
> develop intimate friendships.

How can we say this so confidently when many people, even Christians, seem to lack deep friendships? Because God gave each person the capacity to love—and the command to love. "Dear friends, let us love one another, for love comes from God" (1 John 4:7). And love is the foundation of friendship: "A friend loves at all times" (Proverbs 17:17).

This chapter was meant to liberate you from the overwhelming demands of friendship by defining levels of friendship and their constant variation in terms of time, intensity, and personal capacity. Take a few moments now to examine your own capacity and to identify one or two friendships you would like to develop further.

Summary

1. We can distinguish three primary levels of friendship beyond acquaintances:

Level One—Casual, Level Two—Close (Associate, Personal, Mentor), and Level Three—Intimate or Best. These levels serve to indicate the process of friendship development; they are not fixed categories.

2. We can expand our capacity for intimate friendship by focusing on a few good friends rather than many casual friends.

Principles

1. Close and intimate friendships take time to develop.

2. Friendships will ebb and flow in intensity over time.

3. Everyone has a *limited* capacity for friendship, and each person has a *different* capacity for numbers of friendships.

4. Every person has the capacity to develop intimate friendships.

CHAPTER 3
Why We Need Friends

THE THOUSANDTH MAN

One man in a thousand, Solomon says,
will stick more close than a brother.
And it's worthwhile seeking him half your days
if you find him before the other.
Nine hundred and ninety-nine depend
on what the world sees in you,
but the Thousandth Man will stand your friend
with the whole round world agin you.

'Tis neither promise nor prayer nor show
will settle the finding for 'ee.
Nine hundred and ninety-nine of 'em go

by your looks, or your acts or your glory.
But if he finds you and you find him,
the rest of the world don't matter;
for the Thousandth Man will sink or swim
with you in any water.

You can use his purse with no more talk
than he uses yours for his spendings,
and laugh and meet in your daily walk
as though there had been no lendings.
Nine hundred and ninety-nine of 'em call
for silver and gold in their dealings;
but the Thousandth Man he's worth 'em all,
because you can show him your feelings.

His wrong's your wrong, and his right's your right,
in season or out of season.
Stand up and back it in all men's sight—
with that for your only reason!
Nine hundred and ninety-nine can't bide
the shame or mocking or laughter,
but the Thousandth Man will stand by your side
to the gallows-foot—and after!
(Rudyard Kipling, from A Selection of His Stories and Poems,
edited by John Beecroft, Doubleday, 1956.)

ACH OF US longs for that "Thousandth Man." We want someone who sticks closer than a brother, shares without insecurity, and accepts without reserve. A friend like that is rare, but we all look for one.

Even the person who has learned to live a life of solitude and privacy and who takes pride in independence needs friends. He might say he lacks nothing, but once another person breaks into the closed circle of his life he can see the deep need that had previously lain silent. He is like an undernourished child, who doesn't even know what it's like to feel healthy until he receives the proper food and begins to fill out.

Some find their deepest friendship with their spouse, but even then our need goes beyond this one friendship. We need friends at every level—casual, close, and intimate—to live an emotionally healthy and fulfilled life.

Benefits of Friendship

Friends fill a multitude of needs. Scripture provides varied examples of the benefits of friendship. David and Jonathan enriched each other's lives with a friendship which defied circumstance and position (see 1 Samuel 20). Although Jonathan and David were rivals for the throne of Israel, the bond of friendship drew them together in commitment, and Jonathan willingly sacrificed his inheritance to defend and help David.

Barnabas and Timothy were both co-workers and friends of the apostle Paul. Barnabas was Paul's early sponsor (Acts 9:27), and shared the work in Paul's first missionary journey (Acts 13:1-3). Although they later quarreled and went separate ways (Acts 15:39), both benefited greatly from serving each other.

Paul's relationship with Timothy was that of a mentor as well as a friend. Timothy was Paul's "true son in the faith" (1 Timothy 1:2). Their relationship began as teacher and pupil and developed into intimate friends and co-workers.

We can identify at least eight major benefits from close or intimate friendship.

Emotional encouragement. As we grow in our friendships with others, we develop emotionally supportive ties to them. A good friend builds us up and enriches our self-esteem by letting us know that he accepts and loves us. "Perfume and incense bring joy to the heart, and the pleasantness of one's friend springs from his earnest counsel" (Proverbs 27:9). Friendship builds us up emotionally and gives us encouragement and enjoyment. In contrast, the loss of a friend, either through death or conflict, often sends us into discouragement and depression. Friendship always grows emotional roots.

Help in trouble. "A friend loves at all times, and a brother is born for adversity" (Proverbs 17:17). True friendship continues when we are down and in trouble. A friend stands by us and helps, often at great personal expense. He gives, expecting nothing in return.

Personal stability. Without friends we are rootless, because friends and family form the foundation of a stable life. They keep us from rash decisions and self-centered wanderings, and add a proper focus to our career goals. A superb job cannot compensate for a void in relationships.

Spiritual help and counsel. "As iron sharpens iron, so one man sharpens another" (Proverbs 27:17). Some of our greatest spiritual help comes from friends who care about us deeply enough to speak the truth in love. Our friends should be our greatest spiritual encouragement. When a friendship lacks a spiritual dimension we should question if it is a true biblical friendship.

Freedom of expression. In friendship we can speak openly and freely without fear of condemnation. We can share our feelings even if they lack logic. We know that our friends will listen and even rebuke when necessary.

Protection from loneliness and isolation. Without friends we turn increasingly inward as we grow older. And once we isolate ourselves, breaking out becomes more difficult. Friends will keep us from isolation by forcing us into communication, commitment, and expression. They quench the loneliness that we all fear and often feel.

Love and acceptance. Even the most self-assured person needs love and acceptance. We need to be loved for who we are, not just wanted for what we do. We need to be accepted as we are right now, not just for what we might become.

One man in a large corporation befriended a young engineer. When the engineer resigned, the older man was disappointed and said, "I thought you were on your way up and I wanted to ride your coat tails." Obviously this was no friendship, for it was not based on love and acceptance of the young man's inner person.

In friendship, love and acceptance are given by choice, and they go beyond the biblical injunction to accept everyone as a brother or sister in Christ. The acceptance of a friend springs from a unique inner commitment, and this acceptance is not permissive, but responsible, with encouragement towards personal growth and maturity. In an environment of love and acceptance, even rebuke and confrontation are acceptable. "The kisses of an enemy may be profuse, but faithful are the wounds of a friend" (Proverbs 27:6).

Opportunities to give ourselves to others. We benefit not just from what we *get out* of a friendship, but also from what we *give to* the friendship. We all need to extend ourselves outward and allow others to experience the benefits listed above. We must give to receive; a one-way friendship cannot survive.

Improper Motives

Not every friendship has pure foundations, however. Some people pursue a friendship from selfish motives and take rather than give. Some psychologists maintain that no one *ever* acts from purely altruistic motives, because we rarely give to a relationship without receiving something in return. We do, however, have control in *consciously* establishing our motives for friendship. Here are a few of the wrong ones, which will poison a friendship.

To exploit position. Some people pursue a friendship with another only because he or she is well placed in society or the church. No person of reputation or achievement escapes this danger. Celebrities often develop a distinctly suspicious feeling about people who try to befriend them.

The subtlety of this motive makes exploitation difficult to identify. But if you think that this occurs only with widely-known people, look around you. Every segment of society has its own heroes and people of influence. They may be pastors, doctors, businessmen, or anyone who has influence in some segment of society. At any level, we must guard our motives for associating with people of position. "Do not be proud, but be willing to associate with people of low position. Do not be conceited" (Romans 12:16). We certainly don't mean that friendship with people of position is wrong; they need friends too. But we must carefully examine our motives in pursuing those friendships.

To use power. "It's who you know, not what you know." This remark refers to people who can do something to advance our goals. Under the control of this motive, we cultivate friendships with people of power or influence in order to use them at some future time. The pursuit of such relationships is common to the world of business and politics, but no one wants to be used. The French moralist La Rochefoucauld said in the seventeenth century, "What men call friendship is only a reciprocal conciliation of interests, an exchange of good offices; it is in short simply a form of barter from which self-love always expects to gain something." Certainly no one would consider this a proper foundation for a real friendship.

To get money. Money causes people to do many strange things. The Bible speaks much about its use and its dangers. "The poor are shunned even by their neighbors, but the rich have many friends" (Proverbs 14:20). Money acts like a magnet, and it often taints motives. A true friend does not exploit another for financial gain. Those in Christian work whose ministries depend on others' financial support should exercise a special caution about motives in these relationships.

Selfishness. Selfishness is the root of perhaps all improper motives. When we look after only our own needs in a friendship, we become selfish and self-centered, focusing on what we alone derive from the relationship. Our friendship benefits become great only when they lose the self-centeredness which we attach to them.

Healthy Motives

What, then, are the motives with which we should seek friendship? Basically, they're rooted in the reasons why we need friends:

- to be built up personally
- to grow spiritually
- to give to another person
- to have a mentor
- to be encouraged.

We must learn how to bring friends into our lives, but we must have the proper motives if our friendships are to be both biblical and lasting.

Summary

1. The most important benefits of friendship are:
   emotional encouragement, help in trouble, personal stability, spiritual help and counsel, freedom of expression, protection from loneliness and isolation, love and acceptance, and opportunities to give ourselves to others.

2. Improper motives for building friendship are:
   to exploit position, to use power, to get money, and selfishness.

3. Some healthy motives for building friendships are:
   to be built up personally, to grow spiritually, to give to another person, to have a mentor, and to be encouraged.

CHAPTER 4
Making Friends

There are hermit souls that live withdrawn,
in the peace of their self-content.
There are souls like stars that dwell apart
in a fellowless firmament.
There are pioneer souls that blaze their paths
where highways never ran.
But let me live in a house by the side of the
road and be a friend to man.
("The House by the Side of the Road," Home
Book of Quotations, *Dodd Mead Company, 1967.)*

THIS POEM REFLECTS a willingness to develop lasting, meaningful relationships as well as an openness to befriending others.

New friendships demand a first move from someone. They don't erupt spontaneously, nor do they grow without words and communication. New friendships depend upon one person's willingness to step out and approach another.

But most people do not naturally feel like generating new friendships. Meeting new people, starting conversations, and revealing oneself takes effort and is emotionally draining. Most of us find it much easier to wait for someone else to make the first move.

Well, then, why bother to develop friendships? Most people are as busy as they care to be—busier, perhaps, than they ought to be. Won't it just take more time, demand more effort, and add more pressure? Wouldn't it be easier to maintain just the present demands of life? (And in our fast-paced culture, those demands are considerable.)

The answer is no, for that leads to a selfish concentration on personal schedules and interests. We may be focusing on activities that have little lasting value, while ignoring new friendships that will enrich our lives for years to come. Initiating friendships requires effort and time, but these new friendships pay great dividends.

Old friends, like old shoes, keep us comfortable. But we may become too comfortable with old friends, and withdraw from new relationships. If we start falling into this pattern, we should ask ourselves two pertinent questions: What personal growth and development am I missing by not developing new friendships? and, Do others *need* my friendship even though I may not need theirs?

As you answer these questions, remember that new friends can keep us growing. They will stimulate us in ways that old friends can't. And others need us; they're lonely and need someone to fill that void. For the same reasons we need friends at various times in our lives, others need friends now. We must never lock others out of our current friendships. Leave the gates open. Welcome others into your life.

When we entered the Air Force, one of our first assignments took us to the dry, barren plains of west Texas. We were far from family, friends, and familiar surroundings, and didn't know anyone there.

On our first Sunday we attended services in the base chapel, feeling rather awkward and new. A young couple spoke to us after the service and introduced themselves as Bill and Doris Waldrop.

By the time that week ended, we had been in their home for dinner and had attended a Bible study with them. They were busy people—Bill with a developing career and Doris with young babies and an active participation in the spiritual activities on the base—yet they saw our need for friends and initiated a friendship that continues today.

What if they had not taken the initiative?

We need to leave the door open to new
friends, for their benefit and ours.

Dr. Keith Sehnert, in his book *Stress/Unstress*, states that twenty percent of American families move every year. That statistic means that the average family will move sometime within the next five years. Ours is a mobile society.

Any time we move, we enter new situations, and are then forced to extend ourselves and begin new relationships. Many of these will never progress beyond the acquaintance stage, but some will ripen into fulfilling and lasting friendships.

Friends of ours moved a distance of ten miles, but remained in the same metropolitan area and retained the same jobs. But their move necessitated developing new neighborhood friendships, new church friendships, and, for their children, new school friendships. Although they still occasionally see friends from their old neighborhood and church, for practical reasons they have had to diminish those friendships and establish new ones.

Moves are seldom easy to handle. We cling to the known and the comfortable and view with caution the unknown or strange. But the anticipation of new friends can soften a difficult experience and create a warm response to a new situation.

The Bible records positive examples of people who moved and from necessity developed new acquaintances and friendships.

Joseph was wrenched from his family and homeland and forced to carve a niche for himself among strangers. His ability to establish positive friendships actually led to his opportunity for position and influence in the land of Egypt and friendship with the most powerful ruler of the ancient world (see Genesis 37 and 39–50).

Esther left the familiarity of her uncle's home to live a life among the king's chosen women. Her personality won friends among the leaders of the nation, among the other women, and among her own people.

The apostle Paul itinerated over the whole of Asia Minor, developing deep, lasting, and spiritually-based friendships in every place he stopped.

Jesus made the most dramatic move of all history— from the home of the Creator to the home of the created. Yet he developed friends as a basic characteristic of his lifestyle on earth.

We must all face changes in life. And with life's changes comes the necessity—and opportunity—to develop new friendships. These changes and moves start early in life and continue through old age. We enter public school, then move on to college or a job, career changes, in-laws, geographical relocations, and perhaps eventually a rest home. Without the skill to initiate friendships, these changes can bring loneliness and alienation.

Why We Avoid Initiating Friendships

Although most people know when they can or should try to initiate friendships, many hesitate and miss opportunities. What holds us back from extending ourselves? Why do we often wait for another person to move toward us? How can we recognize the characteristics that barricade us from new friendships? A look at a few possibilities may help us to identify some of the things in our own lives that keep us from making new friends.

Fear of rejection. Any time we make an overture of friendship that is rebuffed or ignored, we feel wounded or unworthy. We have offered ourselves, opened our lives to another, but didn't attract his or her interest. Rejection hurts, and causes us to throw up a defense against trying again.

Perhaps we made an unwise choice of a possible friend or rushed the initiation of the friendship. But too often we accept personal blame for the rejection, when in reality, the other person was unkind, indifferent, rude, uncommunicative, or excessively shy.

Although rejection pains us deeply, it should not be used as an excuse to insulate ourselves. We will deny ourselves the pleasure and joy of future friendships if we retreat from attempts to initiate friends.

When Mary and I moved to a new city and a new church, we began the process of making new friends. I saw one couple to whom we were both attracted. I

made several attempts to get to know the husband, all
of which were received cordially. But nothing ever
developed. We remained casual church friends, but I
never saw any friendship moves in our direction. It
became obvious that this was not a couple God had in
mind for us to develop a closer fellowship with.

In order to maintain the right attitude if someone
rejects your friendship advances, keep in mind this
principle about making friends:

> God does not intend that every friendship
> we attempt to initiate should develop.

If we don't trust God for our friendships, rejection
may become an emotionally damaging experience for us.

Allison entered a Christian college, enthusiastic
about her studies, activities, and new friendships.
Unknown to her, her assigned roommate was attending
because her father would finance her studies only at a
Christian school and not the state university, which was
her first choice.

Allison first met Kate on a hot September afternoon
when they were both tired from the drive to the school and
both dreading hauling their belongings to the fourth floor
of the dormitory.

"Hi," Allison said cheerfully as she entered the room
and found Kate sitting on a suitcase. "I'm Allison."

"Yeah? Well, I'm Kate and this sure is a ratty little
room and I don't know where I'm going to put all of my
things, much less your stuff!"

Over the next several weeks Allison made several
attempts to relieve the strained situation and generate a
friendship with her roommate, but she was always met
with a cutting reply and hostile looks. Finally Allison gave

up, and the stand-off lasted until the end of the school year.

Allison made other friends on campus, but the constant air of rejection and tension made her wary of opening herself to others. Although she was assigned a congenial roommate the following year, it wasn't until her senior year that she fully came out of the shell her freshman year experience had crowded her into.

Rejection may take time to heal. Unless we decide to overlook a few incidents of rejection throughout our lifetime, we will deny ourselves the delight of many possible friendships.

Many times we react negatively to rejection for reasons that aren't even there. What seems like a personal put-down may actually be a response to something that has nothing to do with us. In Allison's case, Kate's rejection of her was not because of anything she was or had done, but because Kate resented and rejected the entire school, which just happened to include Allison.

We can help alleviate our fear of rejection if we understand this principle:

> Rejection of friendship advances does not equal rejection of the person. Many other factors are involved.

Shyness. "He's so bashful," Bruce's outgoing, boisterous mother often told her many friends through Bruce's childhood. "Isn't a bit like me, is he? Must take after his dad's side of the family."

By the time Bruce reached adulthood he believed it. His shyness impeded natural, spontaneous friendships, and for several years he lived on the lonely fringes of groups at his church and on his job. He seldom contributed but appeared to be content to listen and to laugh at the appropriate jokes without participating in the quick, friendly banter around him. He was never openly rejected, but because he was ignored socially, he was denied access to the close friends he longed to have.

Then a young woman began attending his church. Helen always spoke with Bruce, slowly drawing him out of his lonely shell. She listened attentively, and Bruce was always astonished that she remembered their previous conversations and asked him relevant questions.

After several months, others in the church began to notice a change in Bruce. He occasionally contributed to group conversation, even initiating fresh topics. On a hesitant basis, he began to seek out individuals and converse with them much as Helen had with him. For years he had observed other silent and lonely people like himself. With fresh assurance, he resolved to bring some glimmer of friendship to others.

Shyness has two basic manifestations. Some people steer away from social contact with others, even on a friendly basis. They're comfortable with only a few limited relationships, and their shyness prevents a wide range of acquaintances and friends.

The other side of shyness is a refusal to let other people into one's life—a basic fear of letting *anyone* view the inner self. This is different than a natural confident reserve. The shy person experiences anxiety at the thought of allowing others to see him as he really is, fearing he does not have enough to offer.

Both aspects of shyness—avoiding social contacts and fearing self-revelation—seclude the shy person from meaningful friendships. The expression *painfully shy* is no mere figure of speech. Shyness produces loneliness which hurts, and it aggravates doubts about self-worth, which causes acute anxiety.

Overcoming shyness and reaching out toward others may be a long process. In Bruce's case, the answer was simple. He needed an interested, understanding person to make him feel valued and significant. Extreme shyness, however, may require far more time, and even professional counseling, to mitigate its effects.

Those who desire to overcome their shyness and build new friendships need to establish a new outlook on themselves and other people. This process will require determination, time, and energy. It would be very helpful for the shy person to recruit a sympathetic friend to help him through the process—perhaps a close family member or a trusted church acquaintance.

Scripture provides us with two major antidotes to shyness:

1. God has lovingly created every person with valuable qualities—that includes you! If others fail to see your good qualities, don't let that persuade you that you don't have any. "So God created man in his own image. ... God saw all that he had made, and it was *very good*" (Genesis 1:27,31). "I will be glad and rejoice in your love" (Psalm 31:7).

2. We have a responsibility before God to extend our lives to others. "For we are God's workmanship, created in Christ Jesus to do good works, which God prepared in advance for us to do" (Ephesians 2:10).

Don't let shyness keep you from reaching the fulfillment God intends for you in sharing your life with others.

Judgmental attitudes. Erroneous first-impression judgments of people can prevent us from attempting other friendships, and we may find ourselves poorer because of our judgmental attitudes. We have a tendency to look for our own kind, to fit into a comfortable group of people similar to ourselves, and to reject the intrusion of someone different.

Jesus assembled around himself a diverse collection of men who under ordinary circumstances would not associate with each other socially, much less become friends. Common fishermen, a socially ostracized tax collector, and a political zealot were among the twelve that Jesus chose to accompany him. Centered around Jesus, these disparate individuals became friends in a closely-woven group which ultimately fired the world and changed history.

For the most part, we will tend to draw our friends from those of our own age, intellectual development, common interests, and spiritual background. But let's remain open to friendships with widely diverse people.

Poor self-image. Thousands upon thousands of people live isolated, lonely lives because they feel no one could possibly be interested in a friendship with them. After all, they think, what do they have to offer? They possess no special talents, exhibit no glamorous personality characteristics, and have nothing exceptional or beautiful about their appearance. Why would anyone even notice them, much less seek out a friendship?

Our high schools, colleges, neighborhoods, and churches overflow with far too many of these sad, solitary people. Their lack of confidence may be the result of critical, negative parents, personal rejection by friends or colleagues, negative thinking patterns, or unfair comparisons with others. Whatever the cause, a poor self-image impedes friendships and isolates a person behind a wall of pain and dejection.

When we recognize that God has created each of us as a unique person, that we do have God-given characteristics to offer as a friend, we can begin to break the shell of loneliness. Each of us has something to contribute to the life of another.

How to Make Friends

Perhaps you want to initiate friendships and expand your circle of friends, but you're not sure how to make the first move. These practical suggestions may help you.

Create opportunities. In our busy society, most people seem to be caught up in a whirl of activity, and approaching them may seem futile. But many people stay busy to cover their loneliness. Look for opportunities to meet people and to develop an acquaintance that may mature into friendship.

For example, try the Sunday evening service at your church, a Sunday school class, or a small Bible study or prayer group. These occasions are often less formal and smaller in number than the Sunday morning worship service.

You could also attend social events associated with your children's school, your work, and your neighborhood. Sometimes Christians avoid such activities, feeling they may detract from spiritual pursuits, but it is on just such occasions that we can broaden our circle of friends to include Christians and non-Christians alike.

Make friendly overtures to those around you. Learn to feel comfortable with small talk, or as some have called it, cliche conversation. This is valuable for opening communication. Discussions about such topics as your name and hometown, the weather, local events, or government doings ease the initial clumsy moments of meeting. They can pave the way into a more meaningful discussion or allow the conversation to be dropped without any strain on the part of either person.

Take the first step. Jane attended a Sunday school class in friendship evangelism. Although she had been a Christian since childhood, she had never led another person to Christ, and it was something she longed to do.

During the second class, the leader asked each person to make one new acquaintance that week. It would not be a deep friendship, of course, but even the beginning of a casual friendship would be fine.

Jane worked in a large, open insurance office. She noticed another woman who had recently begun work there but didn't enter into the office chatter and banter as most of the other people did. Instead she concentrated exclusively on learning her job, ate lunch alone, and hurried out at the end of working hours.

On Monday morning, Jane walked by her co-worker's desk and said, "Hi, Dottie. Did you have a good weekend?"

Dottie looked up, smiled, and responded briefly.

On Tuesday, Jane asked Dottie to eat lunch with her, and by Friday Jane had discovered much about Dottie's life. She couldn't lead Dottie to Christ because she found Dottie already believed in Christ. She was recently widowed and had moved to be near her parents and worked to support two growing sons.

Dottie was delighted to find a Christian friend, and Jane brought her new friend and family to church with her. Her friendship overtures had been successful.

Dottie might have continued eating her lunch alone if Jane hadn't stepped in. Small gestures of interest and concern may result in solid friendship, but *someone* must make the first move. Friendship needs a starting point—a smile, a greeting, a kind word, an interested question.

When I entered college, I went from a small farming community where I had lived most of my life to a large city. Although I didn't like to think of myself as one, inside or out, I became a shrinking violet.

Because of my long residence in my country

community, I had rarely needed to make new friends. We'd all grown up with each other. When new situations did arise, I allowed my parents or my confident older brother to breech the social gap for me.

However, once I entered a large school in a large metropolis, I realized I had to initiate some friendships or do without friends. I'm chagrined to report that I didn't do very well. It seemed too risky to take those first steps. The result was that if others didn't approach me, they didn't meet me.

But once again I moved, transferred to a huge university, and entered a collegiate church group where the order of the day was "initiate or vegetate." The wise leaders of this group set a relaxed, cordial tone that invited reserved, inexperienced people to venture some friendly overtures to others. And I began to experience the rewards of initiating friendships.

Then I met Jerry—outgoing, assured, positive, and warmhearted. When Jerry met a stranger, that condition didn't last long. He quickly became an acquaintance or a friend. I found it helpful to observe this one-man war against isolation and loneliness. Everyone rated a bit of Jerry's time and a quick word, or even a lengthy talk.

I learned to value contact with people and to appreciate the opportunity to express friendship, concern, and interest in another. You, too, can learn to make the first move.

Be yourself. Attempting to play a role in friendship inevitably leads to trouble. When we initiate a friendship, honesty is a key component. We create problems when we show a new acquaintance a false picture of ourselves. If you are naturally quiet, don't try to be the life of the party.

A big part of an honest friendship is just being our natural selves. We do make some accommodation to any group or person we are with, but we must demonstrate our basic personality and let that be the attraction to another person. And the more that personality is under the control of Jesus Christ, the more appealing that person will be, with positive values most apparent and the rough edges smoothed off.

Form reasonable expectations. When you are developing friendships, avoid hoping for too much too soon. Many people resent a high-pressure approach. Be sensitive to responses. If you perceive hesitancy or withdrawing, hold back and don't strain to make the friendship progress. Everyone needs time and breathing space to feel his way into a new relationship.

Also avoid expecting absolute success in every case. Be willing to advance your friendship even knowing that you may be rebuffed. Rejection is a risk that every friendly person has experienced to some degree.

Allow time for deep friendship to ripen. Friendships built slowly have a lasting foundation; speed need not be a factor. Intimate friendships may take several years to reach maturity. Adjust your expectations accordingly.

We have found that men and women tend to have different expectations for friendship. Although both place great importance on the element of deep sharing, in practice men tend to be satisfied with a lower level of sharing (for example, a relationship that revolves around activities rather than conversations) than women look for. Women may be less tolerant, therefore, when the friendship doesn't live up to their expectations. Keep in mind that these differences may affect the way you make friends, especially if you're developing a couple-to-couple relationship. Stay flexible in your expectations.

Take risks. In the beginning of every relationship someone takes a risk. Even in the best circumstances and with the most congenial people, we take risks as we reach out and extend ourselves. We risk time, embarrassment, and rejection. But it is worth the risk if we open doors to friendships.

We also take risks in social situations. A non-skier hazards the slopes and the possibility of spending half his time lying in the snow to be with friends. Others endure fifteen gutter balls to bowl with friends. Some attend classical music concerts even though they know nothing of music, because it is an evening with a friend.

Learn to take relational risks as well as social risks. Don't allow first impressions to prevent you from pursuing further contact. Some people who are not immediately or naturally drawn to each other can become the best of friends.

Create a sociable environment. In the Seattle area, where we live, some people get depressed because of the constant rain and frequently overcast skies. But others revel in the fertile greenery and mild weather of this coastal climate. Beginning friendships also respond to certain climates. Crowds and courtrooms seldom generate new friends. Small gatherings, however, such as a meal at home, dessert after church, or a Bible study, are informal social environments which provide a good climate for new relationships to grow.

Some people are naturally adept at creating such environments. All of us can do it to some degree. Identify the kind of environment in which you respond well to others, and use it to foster new friendships. Be willing to invite new people to your home and to social activities.

Look for common interests. People are often attracted to each other around common interests and activities. As you interact with people, reach for the common denominators—children, age, hobbies, jobs, neighborhood, or recreation. When you find them, begin to focus on them as the attractive forces between you for the first weeks of your friendship. Branch out to other things later. Be a learner and express interest in their interests. Everyone likes to talk about himself. Listen and learn.

Dale Carnegie, in his classic 1936 work *How to Win Friends and Influence People* (Pocket Books, 1964), listed six rules to make people like you. Consider them as you initiate friendships.

1. Become genuinely interested in other people.
2. Smile.
3. Remember that a man's name is to him the sweetest sound in any language.
4. Be a good listener. Encourage others to talk about themselves.
5. Talk in terms of the other man's interest.
6. Make the other person feel important—and do it sincerely.

These are just helpful social tips, however. Jesus gave us the key to relating to new friends. "In everything, do to others what you would have them do to you" (Matthew 7:12).

Any strong, supportive, enjoyable friendship had a beginning at some point in time. Think now of a satisfying friendship of your own, or one you have observed. You or someone else made the initial movement to get that friendship going. Isn't it worth trying again?

Special Cases

Friendship between couples. Have you ever noticed that it is often more difficult to develop a couple-to-couple friend-

ship than an individual friendship? Often either the men
are close or intimate friends and the wives are not, or the
wives develop a deep friendship and the men remain at the
Level One casual state. Most people who have tried to initiate friendships with other couples have discovered this
principle:

> Developing couple–to–couple friendships is more
> complex than developing individual friendships.

Here is a clue to why this difficulty exists. Only *one*
relationship exists in a person-to-person friendship. But
with couples, look at the combinations (Figure 4-1).

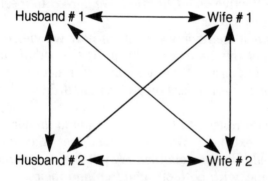

Figure 4-1: Friendship between couples.

Six individual relationships that must function! Is it
any wonder that more care is required to develop couples
relationships? You may wonder why we include the
husband-wife relationship within each marriage. First,
just because they're married it doesn't necessarily mean
they're really good friends. Second, they relate differently
in a couple-to-couple environment than they do by
themselves.

Is the extra effort worthwhile? Most assuredly. We

find great satisfaction in our couples friendships because we share them together. They enhance rather than exclude individual friendships.

When we moved to the Seattle area, we began to pray for one couple with whom we could develop both friendship and ministry. A few months after we arrived, I received a call from Chris Canlis. My name had been given to him by a mutual friend. He and his wife, Alice, had moved back to Seattle a year earlier to take over his father's restaurant business. In our initial phone conversation, Chris rather bluntly said he sensed the need for an accountability relationship to help him be more effective as a Christian. We agreed to meet for lunch to discuss it.

At lunch we reviewed some of how we viewed ourselves at this time in our lives. At the end of our time I said, "Chris, I think you and I can get along fine, but it won't work unless our wives are drawn to each other."

I then arranged to have them come to dinner at our home the next night. We both prayed that Alice and Mary would like one another. We felt the environment of our home, with both our children and theirs, would be the best place for them to see us as we are.

The evening was a pleasure. Chris later reported that Alice sensed a rapport with Mary from the time she came into our home. Since we wanted a deeper friendship, we felt we must be friends as couples, not just individuals. Since that time we have continued to develop our friendship and it has been one of the most satisfying aspects of our move to this area.

What can couples do to foster their relationships with each other? Here are a few key suggestions which you may find helpful. Use them alongside the general suggestions for making friends listed earlier in this chapter.

- Be aware that the relationship is more complex and will take longer to develop. Knowing this will help you as you develop the friendship.
- Couple-to-couple, wife-to-wife, and husband-to-husband friendships need to be developed.
- Recognize that one of the individual friendships will probably develop faster than the others, and will likely be the driving force behind the couples friendship. The other spouses will need to make extra effort to participate in the friendship. (Seldom are the friendships equal.)
- Children's relationships add another complication. Be tolerant of the other couple's children, and occasionally do things including the children rather than always just the four of you.
- Guard against consuming so much of the other couple's time that the friendship becomes oppressive. (One good sign is that you both feel free to do things together on short notice, and you take no offense if your invitation is rejected.) Use the telephone for more frequent, but short, communication.
- Pray together as couples.

Friendship in the discipling process. A final issue which may come up as you seek to initiate friends concerns discipleship. Perhaps the first question we should raise is this: Must an intimate friendship exist between two people for effective discipling to occur?

After much thought, we must respond, *no*. There are many reasons for this. First, the discipler may not have the capacity for another intimate friendship. Second, the one being discipled may not have the capacity. Third, though the communication of truth and the stimulation of spiritual growth is enhanced by intimate friendship, the effectiveness rests on the personal response to God, not to the other person.

Should a discipleship relationship grow into a friendship? Yes. Jesus emphasized the importance of friendship in discipleship when he spoke to his disciples following the last supper.

> My command is this: Love each other as I have loved you. Greater love has no one than this, that one lay down his life for his friends. You are my friends if you do what I command. I no longer call you servants, because a servant does not know his master's business. Instead, I have called you friends, for everything that I learned from my Father I have made known to you. (John 15:12–15)

If we are going to be involved in the great adventure of introducing people into the kingdom of God and supporting them as they become mature disciples of Christ, we must be adept at developing loving friendships. Disciplemaking far exceeds an academic plan or program, though organized methods play a vital part. Rather, discipleship in its fullest sense is one loving member of God's family helping another.

Occasional counseling, biblical teaching, and social fellowship function well in the environment of friendship. But friendship must undergird the process of deep life-on-life influence. The discipleship process may begin with acquaintances, but should always have the goal of deeper friendship. It may not be an intimate level friendship, but rather a close Level Two friendship, which in most cases is both necessary and sufficient. In many cases it will bear the marks of a mentor friendship.

Let us not demand too much of the relationship in

terms of friendship. As has been our experience, some do develop into intimate friends, but others do not. We certainly want to disciple more people in our lifetime than our small capacity for intimate friendship would allow.

Summary

1. We avoid initiating new friendships because of:
   fear of rejection, shyness, judgmental attitudes, and poor self-image.

2. When making new friends, try the following steps:
   create opportunities, take the first step, be yourself, form reasonable expectations, take risks, create a sociable environment, and look for common interests.

Principles

1. We need to leave the door open to new friends, for their benefit and ours.

2. God does not intend that every friendship we attempt to initiate should develop.

3. Rejection of friendship advances does not equal rejection of the person. Many other factors are involved.

4. Developing couple-to-couple friendships is more complex than developing individual friendships.

CHAPTER 5
Keeping Friends

W E MET Roger Brandt on a muggy, hot day in Florida as we stood outside a military chapel following Sunday services. We were immediately attracted to Roger's warm personality, and when we met his wife Joanne two days later we were drawn to her quiet, calm demeanor.

Roger was a new Christian then, and eager for fellowship. Our developing friendship was filled with mutual activities and times of quiet discussion, Bible study, and working together in the chapel program.

Our homes were only two blocks apart, and we would often walk back and forth in the warm Florida sunshine. We'd take the little children to the beach or go shopping together. Joanne taught Mary to sew and we often baby-sat for one another.

After a year and a half of deepening friendship, both Jerry and Roger were scheduled for reassignment. To our surprise and delight we received assignments to the same base in Ohio and realized our friendship could continue on a personal level for another two years.

Roger and Joanne moved first, and we followed a few weeks later. The Brandts were well settled by the time we arrived, but we found that the warehouse where the Air Force had stored our household goods had burned to the ground.

The Brandts stepped in to help. They cared for our children for many days while we started the monumental task of replacing our household goods—everything from a potato peeler to bedspreads to chairs to sit on. They prayed for us and with us during that time. They rejoiced with us that only our possessions were destroyed and that we were not threatened or harmed in any way.

During our assignments in Ohio we attended the same church, traded baby-sitting, picnicked together, and prayed and commiserated together as Roger and Jerry worked toward their master's degrees. We each added another child to our families, and in many ways shared the same struggles and joys.

Over the next several years, we had separate assignments and, to our delight, another mutual assignment in Colorado. We found that not only we, but our children, developed close friendships. During the years when we lived apart, we found that we could continue our friendship by letter and phone. When we were able to visit one another, we resumed our fellowship on the same level.

We consider our friendship with Roger and Joanne a lifelong blessing. We do not know if God will allow our paths to cross so closely again as they did in our early years of friendship, but we do know that each one feels confident and secure with the others. We know God has given us an unusual relationship where the wives have a good friendship, the husbands have a good friendship, and as couples we enjoy a solid friendship.

The Structure of Christian Friendship

We have observed that for Christians, deep and intimate friendships are with other Christians. Although we should also have friendships with non-Christians (see chapter eleven), they cannot attain that qualitative strength that binds Christian friends together.

When the central focus of a relationship is not one another, but Jesus Christ, the friendship reaches depths impossible without that spiritual dimension. The triangular diagram below (Figure 5-1) has often been used to illustrate the relationships between husband and wife and God. The same is true, however, for a lasting Christian friendship. This key principle takes effect:

As both friends draw closer to God,
they also draw closer to each other.

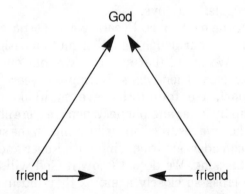

Figure 5-1: The structure of Christian friendship.

When both friends focus on pleasing the Lord, the Holy Spirit begins a work that flows into their friendship. Friendship centered around Christ gives fellowship its full meaning. The apostle John must have experienced this true friendship many times in life when he wrote, "But if we walk in the light, as he is in the light, we have fellowship with one another, and the blood of Jesus, his Son, purifies us from every sin" (1 John 1:7). This active relationship with Christ benefits us personally and extends into our friendships.

When two friends focus on the Lord, they will see life in the same way—in God's perspective. Their value systems will be similar, and their life goals will center around God and his sovereign will for them.

The Ingredients of a Lasting Friendship

This spiritual focus allows several positive things to happen in a friendship. If both friends are growing spiritually, intent on following God and doing his will, several important factors will be a part of the friendship. The strongest and most lasting friendships continue with the infusion of the following qualities.

Spiritual stimulation. In a well-maintained friendship, Christians stimulate each other's spiritual growth. One of the great joys of a close friendship is gaining new insights into Scripture or the Christian life from a friend. This is not formal teaching, but two people discussing common interests in ordinary conversation. A growing Christian will naturally talk about his spiritual life with friends. "And let us consider how we may spur one another on toward love and good deeds. Let us not give up meeting together, as some are in the habit of doing, but let us encourage one another—and all the more as you see the Day approaching" (Hebrews 10:24-25).

No friendship is as satisfying as one in which Christ is mentioned often. This aspect gives joy to a relationship.

My good friend Jean lives a few miles away. We see one another often and speak on the phone frequently. Rarely does an encounter go by when she doesn't bring a fresh thought to my mind about the Lord. She is unaware of how she stimulates me, but is just sharing what is happening in her relationship with the Lord in the daily events of life. This is the way it should be; stimulation cannot be forced or faked. Only a genuine sharing of spiritual things will spur a friend on in his own relationship with the Lord.—(Mary)

"We proclaim to you what we have seen and heard, so that you also may have fellowship with us. And our fellowship is with the Father and with his Son, Jesus Christ. We write this to make our joy complete" (1 John 1:3-4). Note the emphasis that John places on the relationship with the Father and Jesus Christ *first*, then on fellowship with one another.

That is precisely the formula that Jesus used with his disciples. He always urged them to focus on the Father, and it ultimately led them to intimate friendships. In all of his communication with the disciples, Jesus directed their focus to spiritual issues.

After these experiences with Jesus, Peter wrote, "Dear friends, this is now my second letter to you. I have written both of them as reminders to stimulate you to wholesome thinking" (2 Peter 3:1).

That is what intimate Christian friends do for each other—they stimulate the spiritual thinking process. This personal interaction between friends promotes spiritual growth, which in turn leads to deeper friendship.

Prayer. Intimate friends pray with and for one

another. Christian friends who never pray together miss one of the finest ingredients of a Christian friendship —an ingredient that is thoroughly established in Scripture. Jesus taught that prayer is both private and corporate— alone and with others. Each contributes to the spiritual life of a growing Christian. "Again, I tell you that if two of you on earth agree about anything you ask for, it will be done for you by my Father in heaven" (Matthew 18:19).

What do you pray for with your close friend? Have you seen God answer prayers so that you can rejoice together? When did you last pray with a friend?

When did you pray *for* a friend? What needs can you pray about? If you pray with him you will always know what concerns him. What has God done for your friend lately for which you can give thanks?

The apostle Paul was familiar with specific needs and prayed for them often, as his epistles record. Note what he says about prayer for the Colossians.

> For this reason, since the day we heard about you, we have not stopped praying for you and asking God to fill you with the knowledge of his will through all spiritual wisdom and understanding. And we pray this in order that you may live a life worthy of the Lord and may please him in every way: bearing fruit in every good work, growing in the knowledge of God, being strengthened with all power according to his glorious might so that you may have great endurance and patience, and joyfully giving thanks to the Father, who has qualified you to share in the inheritance of the saints in the kingdom of light. (Colossians 1:9–12)

If your mind is ever blank when you kneel to pray for your friends, use one of Paul's prayers for his first-century Christian friends.

*Do you feel free to call a friend and ask him or her
to pray for you? I have three or four friends whom I
call to pray for me during times of stress or particular
need. I know they pray for me regularly anyway, and
are willing and pleased to hear of special needs.
Sometimes when writing a book I will call and ask
them to pray specifically that Satan will be hindered
from interfering and that God will give insight and
freedom in the writing. Or I might ask that they pray
specifically for one of our children. Or for an extra
measure of God's strength or grace for me as I face a
difficult situation. Prayer with an intimate friend lifts
us together into the presence of God and draws us
closer than any other form of communication.—(Mary)*

Accountability. A close Christian friend has the right
and responsibility to hold us responsible for our actions.
Who else will point out things that might be offensive or
wrong? Our spouse or our children may do so, but a friend
provides help from a different perspective.

A friendship must gain stability and depth, however,
before either friend achieves the right to move into the life
of another. We should speak "with wisdom" and provide
"faithful instruction" (Proverbs 31:26). We can't rush in
correcting and exhorting all of our acquaintances, or we
would have no friends at all. We need to know a friend well
enough to determine if what we see is a small irritant or a
deep-rooted problem or sin.

This element of a close friendship must be reciprocal.
"The kisses of an enemy may be profuse, but faithful are
the wounds of a friend" (Proverbs 27:6). "A mocker resents
correction; he will not consult the wise" (Proverbs 15:12).
Close friends will give as well as receive correction, but
neither is easy. Many of us approach friendship with a

"peace-at-any-price" attitude. Or we love our friends so much, we feel they can do no wrong. But we do both our friends and ourselves a disservice when we withhold helpful and loving correction. Sometimes, though, we'll find we can do nothing but pray about an area of need.

I once noticed a problem area in a friend but sensed no freedom to pursue it. Instead I prayed for about a year. Then one day he brought the issue up himself and opened the door for me to share my observations. Friendship is not a hunting license for special weaknesses. When correction occurs, however, this exchange between close friends will strengthen rather than threaten an already strong friendship. There is assurance in knowing that a friend will help us grow and develop. The Holy Spirit corrects us daily, but we may not be sensitive to that correction. So the Spirit may choose to use a friend to point out the error.

A few weeks ago a close friend spoke to me about a habit I have that bothered him. When I am sitting in a meeting, a thought will often come to me of something I must do, someone I should call or write. I keep paper and pencil handy to jot these things down. My friend told me that such a habit is distracting and at times insulting to other people in the meeting, especially to whomever might be speaking. I am sure he is right. Although I'm fully aware of the speaker, it may not appear that way. I know I can trust my friend to share with me again to follow up on this need. Because of our close friendship, I don't feel that I will be on my guard with him. I know he'll tell me if there is improvement, or will again remind me gently if I appear to be distracted. I know I can count on my friend to help me with any kind of need in my life.—(Jerry)

Encouragement and affirmation. This is as important as the exhortation we receive. Stop for a moment and try to recall when you last gave some encouragement to a friend. If you haven't recently, say to someone, "I love you." "I'm so glad you're my friend." "I appreciate you so much. You help me in many ways."

We need encouragement when we're discouraged, when we're under stress, when we've done a job well—in short, all the time. Encouragement gives strength, approval, reinforcement, and courage. It can enable us to do things we never thought possible.

Encouragement can take several forms: appreciation for personal characteristics, sympathy in times of distress or sorrow, support to accomplish something thought impossible, thanks for favors, or personal presence in time of need.

God considers this quality so vital in human relationships that he established it as one of the spiritual gifts. "If it is encouraging, let him encourage..." (Romans 12:8). He also commands us in Hebrews 3:13 to "encourage one another daily."

Mutual encouragement in a friendship prevents many problems because it promotes sensitivity and thoughtfulness. This quality always indicates that one friend is thinking positively of the other. Where encouragement is present, conflict is absent. Encouragement lays a firm foundation for exhortation and correction.

Paul understood the first-century Christians' need for encouragement, and he sent special ambassadors to certain churches.

> Tychicus, the dear brother and faithful servant in the Lord, will tell you everything, so that you also may

know how I am and what I am doing. I am sending him
to you for this very purpose, that you may know how
we are, and that he may encourage you.
(Ephesians 6:21–22)

Tychicus will tell you all the news about me. He is a
dear brother, a faithful minister and fellow servant in
the Lord. I am sending him to you for the express
purpose that you may know about our circumstances
and that he may encourage your hearts.
(Colossians 4:7–8)

Helping and serving. One of the great pleasures of a
close Christian friendship is the privilege of helping one
another. We can find great satisfaction in caring for a
friend in a time of trouble or need.

You might feel that you have such a heavy schedule
and are so burdened that you can't extend yourself in a
helpful way even to your close friends. That's just the time
when you need the privilege of helping and serving
another person.

Develop a sensitivity to the needs of your friends.
Watch for clues. Perhaps they have mentioned something
specific. That often happens in normal conversation—not
a request for help, but just a mention of some need. Maybe
the need can be fulfilled by more prayer, or by a special
gift, or by practical help.

We are friends with a young couple near our home.
They have four small children and their schedule is full of
the daily functions of caring for a large family. But often
when Jeanne hears that we are having a steady flow of
guests for several days, she will bake and cook and bring
boxes of good things to help feed the guests. She often asks
what more she can do to help. Many times she doesn't
even wait to ask, but just appears with help.

The other side of helping is allowing ourselves to be served. The American ideal has been to be self-sufficient and capable—the "bootstrap" approach to living. But we need to rely on as well as serve one another.

A few years ago Jerry left for a month-long trip. The next day in a flurry of activity I began stripping wallpaper from our front hallway. With a bucket of hot water I climbed to the top step of the ladder. After an hour of work, several strips were gone but others hung in long dangling shreds. In an effort to remove one of those shreds, I reached far out from the ladder, which began to fall in a slow arc. On the way down I struck the stairway railing sharply.

Neighbor friends rushed in to take me to the emergency room where five broken ribs were discovered. I needed time and rest to heal them, but the doctor had no recommendations for my bruised dignity! Later that day calls began coming as friends heard of the accident. Friends brought food, sent cards, and assured me of their prayers.

One particular call that day impressed me with the ability of friends to serve and care. We had been meeting regularly in Bible study with four couples and had grown to love them very much. Alice called and said, "We've heard about the accident and we're so sorry. We have hired a painter who will be there in two days to strip the remaining wallpaper and paint the hall. And while he's there, he might as well paint your living room, too."

Two days later an efficient painter, along with two helpers, spent a few hours in our home, leaving it fresh and pleasant. We were so grateful for the loving concern and help of those friends.

Helping and serving in a friendship seals our need for each other and gives us a sense of personal fulfillment and satisfaction.

Having fun together. Christian friendships should be fun. If you haven't laughed with your friend until the tears rolled down your cheeks, perhaps your friendship is missing a special ingredient. God intends that we enjoy the sense of humor he gave us, and we can use it to enjoy one another by allowing fun to permeate our friendships.

Friends must decide between themselves what constitutes fun. What is pleasurable to each one individually? How can they do those things together? Often a friendship will have two widely differing personalities, such as one subdued and the other outgoing. The degree of fun which the friendship contains will largely depend on the blend that these two personalities achieve in enjoyment together.

Recently we invited our friends Chris and Alice and their children to go on a picnic with us. Although we had visions of a picnic straight off the cover of *Better Homes and Gardens,* it didn't turn out that way. The weather turned cold and windy. The only table left in the park was in the shade, far from the water and close to the spot where a dog had polluted the park. We didn't have enough fried chicken and the punch was lukewarm. But we didn't care. We were together. As the wind rose even higher, we beat a hasty retreat to our home, where we finished with a wonderful evening of talking and sharing. We laughed over the "best laid plans" that went astray.

Teamwork in spiritual battle. Have you ever noticed how a unique camaraderie develops between people engaged in a demanding project or effort? It could be teammates on a football squad, planners of a community project, workers in a church building project, or people pulling together after a natural disaster. A classic example is the soldier in battle who depends on others to protect, cover, or support him.

In each of these instances, the focus of attention moves from an inward examination of personal relationships to an outward concentration on a mutual goal of great value. Friendships are best maintained in the midst of the spiritual battle. (Chapter ten discusses the effect on friendship in the church when the congregation focuses on spiritual ministry and outreach.) In all Christian friendships, a working partnership in a common spiritual endeavor, whether encouraging each other to grow in discipleship or reaching out to others in evangelism, will build a deeper foundation than a relationship centered simply on spending time together and talking. Too much self-focus and private sharing leads to introspection and ingrowth. We need to be on the front lines of the spiritual battle, where lasting friendships are made.

Remember that, as we observed in chapter two, friendships will naturally ebb and flow in their intensity. We need to allow each other space. Constant togetherness will ruin any friendship. We must be sensitive to the needs of our friends for privacy and solitude. Henry David Thoreau wrote in his *Journal,* "Friends will be much apart. They will respect more each other's privacy than their communion" (February 22, 1841).

Although a friendship may fluctuate in intensity, there is one quality that never changes—the *dependability* of a friend. When a friendship has been carefully fostered and well maintained over a period of time, it lasts forever. Even though friends may move away or circumstances may temporarily intervene, the friendship can be resumed again with little effort. Quality Christian friendships are strong and lasting.

Summary

The ingredients of a lasting friendship are:
spiritual stimulation, prayer, accountability, encouragement and affirmation, helping and serving, having fun together, and teamwork in spiritual battle.

Principles

As both friends draw closer to God, they also draw closer to each other.

CHAPTER 6

Hindrances to Friendship

FEW PEOPLE WOULD choose to live as a hermit—isolated, alone, uncaring, and uncared for. But many people have become hermits even though they're surrounded by others. They are lonely individuals longing for friendship, but their personality characteristics drive others away. Even while aching for companionship, they eliminate potential friends.

After spending all of her thirty-seven years in a small western town where most of her friends were her family members or her husband's family members, Sue moved to a Chicago suburb. Before moving, she wept on her mother's shoulder declaring, "I'll never have new friends!"

Her mother answered, "Of course you won't just *have* them, Sue. You'll have to *find* them."

For the first few months in her new home, Sue found no new friends. She told herself it was because so many women in her neighborhood worked, the church they attended seemed unfriendly, and no one in this large community had time for anything but his or her own hectic schedule.

But her mother kept writing and asking Sue to tell her about the new friends she had found. Finally, Sue felt compelled to make an overture to someone—anyone—so she would have some news to tell her mother. She had noticed another woman a few doors away who seemed to be at home during the day. One day when the mailman delivered the mail, Sue went out immediately to collect her letters. The other woman was opening her mailbox too.

Sue called a tentative, "Good morning."

The other woman responded, "Hi."

"Nice morning, isn't it?"

"Yes, but it's supposed to be a scorcher by this afternoon."

As she spoke, Sue took a few steps in the other woman's direction. Gradually they moved closer until they met in the middle of the street.

"I'm Sue Morton. We're new here."

"I'm so glad to know you. I'm Sally Brown. We're new here too and I haven't really met anyone yet."

They talked for over an hour, finally moving into Sue's house to continue their conversation over iced tea. When Sally left, Sue immediately wrote to her mother telling her she had *found* a new friend.

Greg's overbearing personality placed him on the fringes of the friendly groups he knew. He loved people, but he persistently tried to change them. He pointed out their faults, offered suggestions for their lifestyles, tried to maneuver their schedules, and planned all activities. He was truly baffled when he realized people avoided him and rarely included him in social events. When he was a little boy his mother had sighed and said, "Poor Greg. He's a leader without followers."

Finally, a sympathetic pastor, observing Greg's overbearing nature, confronted him. Greg was astounded to learn how he had affronted many people. He initially tried to defend himself, saying he had only their best interests in mind. But after serious reflection, he realized how domineering and forceful he was. He resolved to change.

Many months passed before people began to notice the change in Greg. Even then, some of his former acquaintances could not accept the changes as real and would not respond to Greg's overtures of friendship. Eventually, however, he built a new framework of friendships.

Friendship Obstacles

We can't be friends with everyone. No one has the emotional capacity or the time to develop deep friendships with a wide range of people. And because of personality and special interests, we will naturally be drawn to certain people for close friendships.

But we should be attractive enough so that many people want to be our friend. Such idealism usually falls short of reality, however. We create situations and circumstances that erect barriers against developing and maintaining quality friendships. Identifying these problems is the first step in hurdling them. What are some hindrances to strong, lasting friendships?

Failure to recognize our need. In our fast-paced society we are prone to substitute acquaintances for friends. We all know people with whom we play tennis or backgammon, attend church, work, and live in the same neighborhood, but to whom we would never reveal our inner thoughts. Perhaps we consider our spouse friend enough. Or maybe we feel that acquaintances are sufficient for our friendship needs.

In order to make and keep friends, we must recognize that every person needs closeness to another human being. Christians need close friends for mutual sharing, enjoyment, stimulation, and prayer. A true friend knows us well enough to encourage and counsel and correct us. If we fail to see the need of close Christian friends, we will deprive ourselves of this upbuilding, maturing experience.

A friend of ours spent a few years as a chaplain in a large city hospital. One evening a middle-aged woman brought her husband to the emergency room. He was dying of a cerebral hemorrhage. As our friend counseled this woman, he asked if he could call a friend or relative to be with her. She answered that she had no family or friends in the city. And she had lived there eighteen years. What a tragically lonely life she and her husband must have lived, and the woman faced only more loneliness in the future because they hadn't recognized the need to make and nurture friendships.

Every individual needs to be personally convinced of the value of close friendships before he can seek to strengthen and encourage such friendships in his own life.

A lifestyle that's too busy. It's been said that "We are all as busy as we care to be." And that probably means "too busy." Caught in a hectic rush of scheduled activities and programs, we can find ourselves too frantic to make space for the extended leisurely times required to build deep friendships.

You may be caught in circumstances beyond your personal control. Perhaps you have a demanding job or work supervisor, or are burdened with excessive family requirements. Or you may feel that you simply don't have time for deep friendships. You may even fear making time for them. But friendships are worth the adjustments it takes to spend time together. Everyone can find unproductive activities to eliminate or ways to simplify living.

A good way to include friends in your life is to do things together. Instead of planning additional activities for an already crowded schedule, include friends in your essential daily activities and join them in theirs. For example, you could jog together, iron clothes together, picnic together, shop together, attend church together, team teach a Sunday school class, or repair your cars together.

Friends don't need preparations and plans to be together. Spontaneity is one of the great joys of a strong friendship. When busy schedules crowd out friends, simply draw friends into those schedules.

Intolerance. In the musical play *My Fair Lady* (lyrics by Alan Jay Lerner, New American Library, 1956), Professor Higgins encounters frustration whenever events or people fail to measure up to his expectations and standards. His frustrations center chiefly on Eliza, the street girl he is trying to remake into a great lady. At last he can stand it no longer, and he sings to his friend Pickering,

> Why can't a woman take after a man?
> Why can't a woman be like you?
> Why can't a woman be like us?
> Why can't a woman be like me?

These amusing lyrics reveal a serious hindrance to friendship: an intolerance for the habits, activities, personalities, and practices of others. Instead of seeing differences as a zesty addition to friendship, intolerant people recoil from differences, considering them wrongs.

Friendship requires that we give friends space to be themselves and to act according to their own feelings and conscience. When we become irritated and intolerant of people around us, we lose the right to make or keep their friendship. We become difficult to be around and even more difficult to like. Intolerance leads to criticism, which in turn destroys friendships.

Jesus showed an amazing tolerance for people of all backgrounds and peculiarities. When the religious leaders attempted to scorn him, they only revealed a strong point of Jesus' character by saying, "Here is ... a friend of tax collectors and 'sinners' " (Matthew 11:19). It shocked the leaders that Jesus saw value in and claimed friendship with those who had chosen a life different from theirs.

In the life of a Christian, genuine tolerance combined with the love of Jesus Christ will open a wide range of friendship possibilities. It will allow you to cross racial lines, social barriers, age differences, and physical limitations. You will accept personality quirks and failings. A tolerant Christian sees every individual through God's viewpoint—as worthwhile and valuable.

Selfishness. A brief appraisal of the magazine counter at your local store will reveal the strong trend toward selfishness which pervades our culture. Such magazine titles as *Me, Self,* and *Us* are examples of our culture's drift toward personal gratification and away from giving and serving. Even Christians can be drawn into this devastating way of thinking.

The very word *friend* implies giving. The root of our word *friend* is the Old English *freon,* which means "to love." Loving in the biblical sense means to give fully by concentrating on the needs, desires, and pleasures of the one loved. If either friend concentrates only on himself, the friendship will weaken and die. One person cannot bear the entire responsibility for the loving maintenance of a friendship.

Little children who are blatantly selfish endure pointed rejection from other children. The same thing happens on an adult scale, only with more subtlety. If a person persists in hoarding his time, his possessions, and the conversations and attention of others, he will find himself friendless.

One of our friends moved with her husband into a new neighborhood. Her next-door neighbor welcomed her warmly, and a friendship began to grow. After several months, the neighbor's husband was assigned to a new job, which required many days of travel each month. In her loneliness, the neighbor began to lean on our friend for support. She would arrive early in the morning with two little children in tow and remain until lunch. She would return home only to give her children a nap, and then would show up again for several more hours.

After several weeks of this routine, our friend became frantic. She tried to do her housework and care for her children in spite of the constant presence of the neighbor and her rowdy children, but she dreaded hearing the early ring of the doorbell. Gentle hints received no response.

Finally, after much prayer and thought, our friend went to her neighbor's home and said in a loving way, "You must build your own life. I know you are lonely, but staying with me every day is not the answer. You must deal with your situation and learn to live with it. I, too, need time alone in my home and with my own children. Our friendship is being ruined by too much time together."

The neighbor began to cry as she recognized her selfishness. After a good talk the women agreed to let their relationship return to a normal pattern.

Criticism. Tom enjoyed being with people, but he sensed they avoided him. And indeed they did, for he rarely contributed to a conversation without criticizing something or someone. He seemed expert at injecting a negative tone into a positive conversation. He often criticized the weather, his job, his church, his pastor, politicians, his family, traffic, vacations, or anything within the range of his thinking or his vision.

Eventually his wife threatened to move out unless he stopped criticizing her. They found a Christian counselor who began to talk with them together and individually. Tom was confronted with the fact that when he criticized, he questioned God's sovereignty. God was in charge of the weather, daily situations, the life of the pastor, and all of the other items that Tom had felt free to find fault with. He was given the antidote for hypercritical people—applying 1 Thessalonians 5:18: "Give thanks in all circumstances, for this is God's will for you in Christ Jesus."

Tom's critical attitude diminished slowly. The habit had become so ingrained over the years that he didn't realize what he was doing, and several months passed before he developed a conscious realization of how often he was tempted to criticize. Two years after he had first been confronted with his problem, he visited a cousin he had not seen in years. After an hour or two of conversation his cousin looked at him quizzically and said, "Tom, you've changed." Tom was able to explain the work that God had done in his life.

Friendship cannot grow or expand in the uncomfortable, depressing atmosphere of criticism. An occasional helpful suggestion, lovingly given, is not criticism. But constant faultfinding does reveal a critical attitude, and it will ruin any relationship.

Criticism stems from a variety of roots—a poor

self-image, an angry spirit, faulty comparisons, or a misunderstanding of God's direction in our lives. Often criticism is just a habit picked up from the way the world complains.

Jesus provided the perfect solution for critical people—*love*. Not just for our neighbors or friends, but even for our enemies (Matthew 5:43–44). Love leaves no room for criticism. The apostle Paul reinforced Jesus' teaching when he said, "Love keeps no record of wrongs" (1 Corinthians 13:5). Therefore, one who loves does not remember things to criticize.

Insensitivity. Some people seem oblivious to the needs of others. They bypass signals that reveal if a friend is depressed, fatigued, troubled, fearful, or irritated. On the other hand, they may be nonchalant when a friend experiences joy, achievement, or success.

Bill burst into his office one morning and, beaming, announced to his friend and colleague, "I'm a grandfather! My daughter Marion had a baby last night!"

Without looking up from his desk, Bill's co-worker replied in a flat tone, "Yeah? good," and went on with his work.

Bill's smile faded, his shoulders sagged, and he slumped behind his desk. That thoughtless response had completely demoralized him.

Insensitivity is behaving towards friends with indifference, unconcern, a lack of feeling in our response, and calloused attitudes. Perhaps it was to people with these characteristics that the apostle Paul offered the advice, "Rejoice with those who rejoice; mourn with those who mourn" (Romans 12:15). God wants us to be alert and caring about our friends, and tuned in to their feelings and their needs.

When people meet with indifference in their friends,

they rarely stop to analyze what might have caused the indifference. They usually interpret the action as rudeness or dislike and tend to avoid the relationship. Then the friendship breaks.

A good friend *always* strives to make friends feel special, to be alert during their time together, and to be thinking about them during their time apart. A friend needs to feel he is one chosen among many.

Jealousy. "Anger is cruel and fury overwhelming, but who can stand before jealousy?" (Proverbs 27:4).

No friendship can continue in a climate of jealousy. Jealousy destroys trust, affection, and freedom between friends. Jealousy reveals a possessive envy and an unwillingness to share the joy of the friendship with anyone else.

Jealousy is listed in Galations 5:20 as one of the acts of the sinful nature. Its consequences truly place it with other destructive acts of sin.

Jealousy in friendship can erupt in several situations: when one friend achieves success or recognition, begins to spend time with another person, or sees the friendship decreasing and tries to hold on.

Stan and Reilly had been friends since high school. They attended the same college, settled in the same city, and continued their friendship as their careers developed and their families grew.

When they were in their forties, Stan made an astute investment that reaped high financial profits and at almost the same time received a large inheritance. Although he gave generously to his church and to missions, Stan's increased income made a noticeable change in his lifestyle. His children had privileges that were impossible before. He and his wife traveled and purchased a new home.

Reilly rejoiced with Stan initially, but as the months passed and he realized that he could never give his family the advantages that Stan's family now had, a deep jealousy began to settle on him. He avoided contact with Stan, who was bewildered but didn't press the issue. After a year or two, they rarely spoke.

Jealousy threatens budding friendships and ruins existing ones. Protect your valued friendships from the invasion of this destructive force.

Frequent moves. Careers or circumstances that require frequent moves may hinder the formation and growth of friendships. One businessman commented on this problem, "Well, I've got the solution. I just don't make friends anymore."

But of course, that merely avoids a solution. Don't get trapped into thinking that forming friendships isn't worth the brief benefit, or that the pain of separation is too uncomfortable to experience again.

Early in our married life we spent nearly fourteen years in the Air Force. The training period and subsequent assignments required many moves. We soon felt the strain of making friends and then being wrenched away. We became more selective in picking our friends and tried to steel ourselves against the separations.

Then we found that the joy of finding friends and the pain of separating from them were normal growth experiences of life. A little geographical distance from friends allowed us to see the precious quality of that friendship and to treasure more wholly the times when our paths would cross again. Some friendships faded in months or a year or two. But many lasted for years and continue today. The quality and durability of the friendships were tested by separation.

Unrealistic expectations. You may be a perfectionist

by nature, easily annoyed by the failings and flaws you observe in people. You would rather avoid friendships than put up with imperfect friends. Or you may have found a friend you admired, but he failed to meet your expectations and disappointed you.

Acceptance is a necessary part of friendship. Every human being is flawed in some way and will fail to meet a perfect standard. Only Jesus was perfect. But even he did not meet the expectations of all of the people around him.

As much as we love our friends and as highly as we regard them, we must allow them room to fail and to show their weaknesses. If we enter friendships realistically, we will spare ourselves considerable disappointment.

Betraying confidences and gossiping. Gossiping about one friend to another is a blow from which few friendships recover. In chapter one, we identified loyalty as a key to friendship. Betrayal is the opposite of loyalty. Telling something shared in confidence devastates the trust established between friends. Without that trust and confidence, communication can only be superficial, and the friendship dies. And it's usually an abrupt and painful break. Rather than allowing the friendship to die slowly, the betrayed friend angrily severs the friendship.

The book of Proverbs amply warns against this kind of gossip: "Do not betray another man's confidence, or he who hears it may shame you and you will never lose your bad reputation" (25:9-10). "A gossip betrays a confidence, but a trustworthy man keeps a secret" (11:13). "A gossip betrays a confidence; so avoid a man who talks too much" (20:19).

Gossip takes two forms: telling lies about another person (technically called slander), or repeating a confidence to a third party. Both of these actions are sin and crush a friendship.

Kathy and Bill Miller had been married nine years before they found out they were going to have a child. In a rush of joy and excitement, Kathy called her best friend Rochelle.

"Rochelle, I just had to tell someone the good news. We're going to have a baby!"

After they had rejoiced and cried together over the phone, Kathy added, "Rochelle, please don't mention this to anyone yet, because Mom and Dad get back from their trip next week and aside from you, I want them to be the first to know."

Within the next two days, however, Kathy received phone calls from four people who expressed their happiness over her news. Finally, Kathy called Rochelle and demanded an explanation.

"I know I shouldn't have, Kathy," Rochelle explained. "But I just couldn't hold back the good news."

Kathy said a cool good-bye and their friendship nearly died. After a long session of confrontation, forgiveness, and tears, their friendship began to revive.

That gossip conveyed truthful, happy news, but betrayed a confidence. How much more devastating when the gossip contains lies or damaging news!

Resolve to be absolutely trustworthy with any information shared with you. If you have any question about sharing it, keep it to yourself. Reject gossip from others, even when offered in the form of a prayer request. Gossip detracts from our relationship with the Lord and it destroys valued friendships. Why get involved?

The following chart lists indicators of possible obstacles to friendship in your own life. If any of these qualities frequently or almost always characterize your behavior, review these needs for change in your life. Resolve with God's help to begin correcting these areas.

I AM . . .	RARELY	SOMETIMES	FREQUENTLY	ALMOST ALWAYS
SHY				
BOSSY				
OVERSCHEDULED				
ONE WHO BETRAYS CONFIDENCES				
ANGRY				
NEGATIVE				
CRITICAL				
DEMANDING				
POSSESSIVE				
UNREALISTIC IN EXPECTATIONS				
UNWILLING TO REVEAL SELF				
PROUD				
INTOLERANT				

Summary

The principal hindrances to developing or maintaining friendships are:

failure to recognize our need, a lifestyle that's too busy, intolerance, selfishness, criticism, insensitivity, jealousy, frequent moves, unrealistic expectations, and betraying confidences and gossiping.

CHAPTER 7

Healing Wounded Friendships

F RIENDSHIPS ARE FRAGILE. They do break. It seems unfair that a friendship made at a great cost of time and emotional energy should crack and split in a moment, but it happens. A harsh statement, an unfair criticism, or a thoughtless action can create a chasm of hostility and hurt feelings which results in separated friends.

Then comes the uphill task of closing the gap and restoring the friendship. Reconciliation can be difficult, since hurt friends often tend to withdraw emotionally. King Solomon recognized the difficulty of mending friendships when he wrote, "An offended brother is more unyielding than a fortified city, and disputes are like the barred gates of a citadel" (Proverbs 18:19).

If that is the case, can a broken friendship ever be

healed? Of course. Eventually, fortified cities do fall and barred gates do open, but only after much time and energy is expended.

We've become accustomed to watching television comedies where relationships are broken and then miraculously mended and the offenses forgotten, all in the space of thirty minutes or less. But rifts in a real friendship heal slowly.

Life is more complex and realistic than it appears in television programs. Broken friendships always create sadness and regrets. If no attempt is made to heal the break, the wound goes on for a lifetime.

We are not talking of those friendships that die a natural death. Usually, those are casual friendships which fade for a variety of valid reasons, such as geographical separations or new circumstances—marriage, a new community, or a new job. They disappear without rancor or hard feelings when situations change. This is especially true of Level Two associate friendships, and Level One casual friendships. The most obvious changes come as young people leave high school or college and move into a new phase of life. For a time they make periodic efforts to keep in touch with old friends, but after a few years pass, they rarely see more than one or two friends from their previous situation.

When we speak of broken or wounded friendships in this chapter, we are referring to those that result from disputes and discord. These friendships need healing and mending. Bitter words cannot be forgotten without forgiveness. Quarrels don't mend themselves. Restoration requires initiation by one person and cooperation from both friends.

Conflicts can build for a long time, or they can erupt suddenly in a furious quarrel. Have you ever had a pleasant conversation with a friend, talking of inconsequential things, when abruptly you inwardly took exception to some statement? Suddenly, all of your senses were alert as you planned a rebuttal. In surprise, your friend listened to your attack. He really didn't have a strong basis for his statement, but since you challenged him, he felt obligated to defend his careless remark. After all, it can be humiliating to have to back down and admit error.

Proverbs pictures the cascading effect of a quarrel. "Starting a quarrel is like breaching a dam; so drop the matter before a dispute breaks out" (Proverbs 17:14). Further in the same chapter Solomon spares no words in defining the seriousness of quarrels. "He who loves a quarrel loves sin" (Proverbs 17:19).

Potential Sources of Conflict

Perhaps Solomon's life in a complex household led him to pen many proverbs on the destructive aspects of conflict. He must have been called on many times to mediate quarrels among his many wives! Certainly pride and jealousy must have initiated quarrels again and again. Solomon recognized this source as he said, "Pride only breeds quarrels" (Proverbs 13:10).

What emotions and actions cause conflict?
- Pride
- Anger
- Envy
- Gossip
- Indifference
- Neglect
- Jealousy

Often a combination of these problems works together to cause conflicts and separate friends.

Ron and Pete had been friends for several years. They

attended the same church, played tennis weekly, and brought their families together about once a month for fellowship and fun. Their relationship was congenial, until one evening a fight erupted between two of their children. Pete verbally lashed out at Ron's son. This led to a discussion on discipline, in which Pete shared a number of negative observations on the way Ron raised his children. Stormy words were exchanged, but they soon left the topic. At the end of the evening Pete said, "Ron, I'm sorry about my criticism earlier this evening."

"That's okay, Pete. Forget it."

But Ron didn't forget it. He brooded about it. He thought Pete was completely wrong in the way he disciplined his children. Pete's child was at fault in the quarrel too. In fact, he had seen some things in Pete's children that were objectionable.

They kept playing tennis and having family get-togethers, but their relationship began to cool. Soon Pete and Ron were making excuses for their time together. Both men sensed that not all was well between them.

One Sunday after church the teacher of the twelve-year-old boys asked to talk to Ron. He shared some of the difficulties they were experiencing with Ron's son in the class. He asked for Ron's help in the problem. Ron was stunned. These were the same issues Pete had mentioned.

He struggled inwardly for several days. Finally he called Pete.

"Pete, this is Ron. Can we get a cup of coffee? I need to talk to you."

Later they met and Ron said, "Pete, I'm really sorry. I've been angry with you for what you said about our son and the way we are training him. But you were right and I just refused to see or admit it. I really appreciate the risk you took to try and help me."

"I knew things weren't right between us," Pete said. "I was wrong in the way I brought it up. I had been thinking about it, but I lost my temper and said it wrong. Will you forgive me?"

They prayed together and agreed to rebuild their relationship.

How to Restore a Broken Friendship

In mending wounded friendships, several steps lead to healing.

Determine the source of conflict. "Make every effort to live in peace with all men and to be holy; without holiness no one will see the Lord. See to it that no one misses the grace of God and that no bitter root grows up to cause trouble and defile many" (Hebrews 12:14–15). We cannot live in harmony when problems exist, and therefore we need to know where those problems come from.

In order to determine what caused a conflict, we should check ourselves with the following questions:

- Have I knowingly spoken harshly or unjustly to a friend?
- Have I neglected contact because of a rushed schedule?
- Does my friend have problems about which I am indifferent?
- Do I ignore a friend when someone more interesting comes along?
- Have I failed to defend my friend when I have heard him or her attacked?
- Do I avoid friends if they are in trouble, in sorrow, or sinning in a noticeable way?

All of these attitudes and actions can wound a relationship. When you sense or observe a friendship in conflict, you can be sure that healing is needed. Too often we are willing to settle for an uneasy stand-off rather than press through the painful process of honest confrontation and resolution.

The first move, then, must be to determine the source of the conflict. This is essential in order to restore peace and growth to a friendship. Conflict left unresolved escalates into bitterness, gossip, or anger, and inevitably draws others into the dissension as well.

Once we know how a conflict started, how can it then be cleared?

Initiate restoration. Jesus taught that where there are problems, conflicts, and offenses, solutions are possible. For whether we have given or received offensive words, we are responsible to initiate restoration.

> Therefore, if you are offering your gift at the altar and there remember that your brother has something against you, leave your gift there in front of the altar. First go and be reconciled to your brother; then come and offer your gift. (Matthew 5:23-24)
>
> If your brother sins against you, go and show him his fault, just between the two of you. If he listens to you, you have won your brother over. (Matthew 18:15)

Have you offended a friend? Has he or she hurt and offended you? Remember, you bear the responsibility for restoring the relationship. Whether you are at fault or your friend is at fault, be willing to risk a further breach in the friendship by trying to settle the issue. Be willing to make peace, even if it means humiliation or rejection. "Blessed are the peacemakers, for they will be called sons of God" (Matthew 5:9).

Jesus knew the inevitability of conflict, but he promised blessing to those who were willing to work toward peace and harmony. In biblical terms, peace is not the *absence* of conflict, but the ability to *confront and heal* broken friendships, however difficult and lengthy that process might be. "Love and forgiveness are costly, but they are the price of good relationships" (from a devotional letter by Concern Ministries Inc. in McLean, Virginia).

Keep short accounts. Restoration is easiest while the offense is still recent. If grievances accumulate, restoration becomes more difficult, and sometimes impossible. A person who has brooded for weeks over a matter may attempt to correct it with tight lips and clenched fists. But if an offense is faced quickly, it is much easier to approach a friend with kind words and a steady tone.

We do not think you should necessarily correct an offense in minutes or even hours, but weeks should not elapse. A short period of time will help prevent impulsive or excessively emotional reactions. "Get rid of all bitterness, rage and anger, brawling and slander, along with every form of malice. Be kind and compassionate to one another, forgiving each other, just as in Christ God forgave you" (Ephesians 4:31–32).

Go in an attitude of humility. Once you've discovered why the conflict occurred and you're ready to initiate restoration, find a time to talk privately with your friend. It should be in a comfortable setting, as free from interruptions as possible, and without time constraints. Decide beforehand to accept all responsibility for the quarrel, to listen to words *and* meanings carefully, and to ask for forgiveness without placing blame.

Some people cannot ask for forgiveness without excusing their bad behavior or unkind words. They approach an offended friend by saying, "I'm sorry I called you a puffed-up bigot, but *you* made me so mad that I just couldn't help it." Such an apology only adds fuel to the fire and can never restore a wounded friendship.

If you have given offense, you might approach a friend saying, "I am truly sorry for losing my temper last Wednesday and saying those harsh words to you. I value our friendship very much and don't want anything to harm it. Will you forgive me?"

Or, if you have been hurt by a friend, you might say, "Yesterday, when we were having lunch, you made jokes about my weight, calling me fat. I've been working hard to lower my weight and I was hurt by your jokes. I don't want our friendship to be threatened by things like that."

If you sense only a strain rather than an overt offense, you could say, "Lately, I have felt uncomfortable about our friendship. Our conversation seems to be strained. Have I offended you in any way? If I have, I really want to make it right and to have your forgiveness."

"An apology is a friendship preserver, an antidote for hatred, never a sign of weakness; it costs nothing but one's pride, always saves more than it costs, and is a device needed in every home" (quoted in *Readers Digest*, April 1979, page 56).

Remember as you ask for forgiveness that your friend, or you, may commit the same offense again and again. Jesus recognized this frailty in human nature, for he talked with Peter about unlimited forgiveness: "Then Peter came to Jesus and asked, 'Lord, how many times shall I forgive my brother when he sins against me? Up to seven times?' Jesus answered, 'I tell you, not seven times, but seventy-seven times' " (Matthew 18:21–22).

We need to be willing to confront and forgive again and again and again as our friends, and we, go through the maturing growth process God intends for us in our friendships.

Allow time to heal. Time is an important factor in healing wounded friendships. It takes time for trust and confidence to rebuild and grow. Time allows friends to feel secure with each other again, and to place some space between them and the difficult time of confrontation. Time is truly a healing factor.

Above all, pray. Another important element of healing is prayer. Pray for full recovery of the relationship. Pray for your personal attitudes, and for your friend to have the right attitudes. Pray against a repeat episode. Trust God to work in and strengthen the friendship, and thank God when the friendship has been healed.

Although confrontation following a quarrel makes us uneasy, or even frightened, certainly the risk in confrontation is preferable to living with conflict, or with anger and bitterness against a friend who may not even be aware of his offensive behavior.

Venture a confrontation the next time you experience a conflict. By following biblical guidelines for resolution, you will save a friendship, please the Lord, and possibly move the friendship to a much stronger basis.

Unfortunately, however, not every friendship comes back together again. Even when attempts are made, some never return to their original closeness. Have you ever tried to straighten a wire clothes hanger? Those corners never seem to get perfectly straight—they always leave an impression on the wire. Some friendship breaks are like that. No matter how we try, we can never quite get them straightened out. We wish it were different, since ideally every relationship is capable of mending. This certainly is true scripturally. But even with resolution of individual problems, the fullness of the friendship may not return. The biblical requirement is to resolve the conflict, not necessarily to restore the same depth of friendship. Friendship is fragile. Handle it with care.

According to Carl Sandburg, an elderly woman asked

Abe Lincoln, "How can you speak kindly of your enemies when you should rather destroy them?"

"Madam," he said, "do I not destroy them when I make them my friends?" (quoted in *Reader's Digest*, December 1980, page 144).

Has a friend become an enemy—at odds, angry, offended? Make him a friend again.

Summary

1. Aspects of our behavior that are most likely to cause conflict in friendship are:

pride, anger, envy, gossip, indifference, neglect, and jealousy.

2. Take these steps to heal a wounded friendship:
Determine the source of conflict.
Initiate restoration.
Keep short accounts.
Go in an attitude of humility.
Allow time to heal.
Above all, pray.

CHAPTER 8
Marriage Friends

"**B**ELOVED, WE ARE gathered together in the sight of God and this company to unite these friends as husband and wife."

If we heard this statement opening a marriage ceremony, we would immediately know the standard lines had been altered. Upon reflection, however, we would see that such a statement makes sense. Marriage should be built on a growing friendship. People who marry strangers (those who aren't deep friends) take a risk.

Too many people, Christians included, marry because of physical attraction. This overrules other considerations, such as intellectual, emotional, and social compatibility, which at the time seem mundane. Then after the flurry of wedding preparations, ceremony, and honeymoon dies down, they discover a depressing fact. Flowing hormones won't sustain a marriage over a long period of time. If the marriage is to flourish, they must establish a durable, enjoyable friendship to undergird their relationship.

The Need for Husband-Wife Friendship

Alan and Beverly experienced the need to develop their friendship after marriage. They met in June just after graduating from college. An acquaintance introduced them after a morning church service. They dated that evening, just before Beverly left town for two weeks to visit her family in a nearby state.

When she returned, she and Alan dated nearly every night for two weeks and then they decided to marry. Shortly after that, Beverly left for her hometown to prepare for the wedding at the end of August. After a brief honeymoon they settled into married life. They soon realized, however, that while they found each other attractive, they really didn't know each other at all. In order to deepen their relationship and give their marriage fullness, they realized they had to develop a friendship with each other.

Recently my mother died after a sudden and brief bout with cancer. As my Dad and I sat on the couch the next day, he shared painfully how much he missed her. He said, "Well, the matter is, we got along so well." Not only were they marriage partners, they were best friends. What a great memory. And what a compliment to their relationship.—(Jerry)

How disheartening it would be to endure years together without real friendship as an expression of love. The friendship we experience in marriage should be the strongest, most fulfilling friendship of a lifetime. It should sustain us through difficult times, and give mutual joy in the happy experiences of life. The more close and precious that friendship becomes, the more carefully we must guard it from devastating influences.

A Special Case

God intended that husband and wife be best friends, but he designed the marriage with complexities that no other friendship encounters.

Sexual intimacy. "For this reason a man will leave his father and mother and be united to his wife, and they will become one flesh" (Genesis 2:24).

Submission and authority. "Wives, submit to your husbands as to the Lord. For the husband is the head of the wife as Christ is the head of the church, his body, of which he is the Savior" (Ephesians 5:22-23).

Other complexities are mutual child rearing, intimate yet sometimes mundane daily living together, financial interdependence, and daily demands for communication.

Why Some Marriages Lack Friendship

Perhaps because of the factors that God built into a marriage friendship, problems seem magnified when they do arise. Certain problems seem to give particular trouble to a marriage friendship.

Excessively physical focus. An overemphasis on the physical aspects of marriage in the early years can push aside a developing friendship. Of course, physical intimacy is an important factor, indeed, a motivating factor in experiencing the exuberant joy of marriage, and God intended that it be so. In no way should sexual discovery and enjoyment be diminished. If the marriage rests on that factor alone, however, it cannot grow to the fullest. From courtship days, a developing friendship should be a central ingredient of the relationship.

Lack of intellectual and emotional interaction. We live in such a fast-paced environment that sometimes husbands and wives find they have no time to communicate except on the most functional level of daily living.

"Can you take Sue to her piano lesson?"

"What time will you get home from work?"

"Remember to renew your driver's license."

"There's a big sale at the shopping center."

Communication like this is essential to a relationship. We can't function without it. But it doesn't reveal feelings or thoughts. It does not draw husband and wife together in intimate communication. To enter that realm of interaction takes time, interest, and privacy.

We need to work hard, in fact, at stimulating communication of the mind and heart. If this is not a part of your life with others, it will not come easily in marriage. Too often we retreat into the easy zone of functional conversation.

Taking each other for granted. Another block to marriage friendship builds when one or both partners takes the other for granted. What does that phrase mean? It defines a pattern of presuming on the love and faithfulness and tolerance of the other partner. Taking another for granted means that there is a selfish concentration on personal needs with a lack of consideration for the thoughts and needs of the other person.

Television's Archie Bunker is a perfect example of the partner who takes his spouse for granted. He roars home from work expecting his dinner immediately. He wants his wife to cater to his whims, moods, and needs. He fails to recognize her thoughts or needs. He never imagines that she might have ideas differing from his own, or, for that matter, any ideas at all. He expects her constant presence and attention. He denies her the affirmation and appreciation every spouse needs. In short, he takes her for granted.

Unresolved day-to-day conflict. Any kind of conflict deals a severe blow to the marriage relationship when friendship does not provide a basis for resolution.

Why do we often feel at liberty to place the stress of conflict on the marriage friendship? Maybe because we are legally bound together and our spouse (friend) cannot easily desert us. But certainly that is a weak excuse for straining the most important friendship we have.

We may also feel that we should be able to vent our frustrations on someone, and certainly our partner should love us enough and be tolerant enough to serve us in that way. But that, too, strains a marriage friendship.

Some issues require serious discussion because of genuine differences of opinion. Marriage partners usually come from divergent backgrounds with different habits, customs, values, ideals, prejudices, and patterns of living. These differences can lead to conflict unless they are calmly and lovingly discussed. A healthy respect for other views is absolutely vital to reducing conflict in marriage.

Many couples truly love one another and desire to have a loving relationship. Even though they want to be best friends, however, they are so plagued by small irritants that they don't like each other very much.

Much conflict, perhaps most, is based on a selfish determination to prove a point or to have one's own way— to be the "winner." And much of it erupts over nonessentials. Who cares whether he hangs his jacket over a chair instead of in the closet? A wife who has been taught to venerate tidiness cares, that's who! What difference does it make if she is usually five or ten minutes late when they are going somewhere? It makes a big difference to a husband who strongly believes in absolute punctuality. And by such conflicts is a good marriage friendship tested.

The Basis for a Marriage Friendship

Building a strong marriage relationship takes time. The process must begin during courtship and continue throughout a lifetime of marriage. The basis of friendship in marriage contains several key elements.

An early start. It is easy for courting couples to become so preoccupied with the delights of being together that they fail to reveal themselves as they might to a friend. They are strongly tempted to present only the very best qualities, to refrain from subjects that will cause conflict, and to acquiesce in periods of potential disagreement in order to maintain harmony. But "peace at any price" won't foster a secure marriage. Learn to communicate honestly early in the friendship.

Some couples swing to the other extreme in courtship, however, and ignore the pleasure of just being together in order to focus exclusively on issues. This approach will not develop a lasting friendship, either.

Several years ago an engaged couple came to us for help in their relationship. They asked us for suggestions on what to discuss before marriage. They had already compiled a formidable list including furniture preference, vacation styles, family size, birth control, and so forth. They asked us to contribute to their list.

We asked them if they were having fun and enjoying each other. They looked at each other for a long moment and then he answered, "No, we really don't have much fun together, but we do want to have a good basis for marriage and get all of these things worked out."

We suggested that they lay aside the list for a few months while they just enjoyed each other's company. If the topics came up naturally, fine—discuss them—but concentrate first on developing the friendship naturally. Eventually they covered many of the topics on their list, but a strong and loving friendship was their first goal.

Lifetime commitment. Another essential for a good marriage friendship is mutual commitment. We need to enter marriage committed to each other for a lifetime, without thoughts of alternatives or escape.

In the fine film, *Strike the Original Match*, Chuck Swindoll's wife relates frustrations she experienced in her marriage. Her motivation to work through the problems came in part from the fact that she had "no options." She entered the marriage with a *lifetime commitment* and divorce was not an option for her.

We all need that conscious commitment. We should verbalize it to our partners. That commitment makes a friendship easier. It can then withstand assaults without fear of breaking.

In an ABC television production, "Summer Solstice" (1979), an aging couple reflects on their life together. They review their wedding scene in flashbacks. They disagree over the phrasing of the vows, and after a lengthy discussion they agree to take one another "as is." Not a bad beginning for a marriage friendship. Later they discuss why he returned to her after marital difficulty. He thinks for a long time and then says quietly, "Because of our vow."

Mutual commitment gives stability, ease, and confidence to a marriage. It provides a climate of healthy trust. Commitment allows a free exchange of ideas and preferences without fear of rejection or desertion.

Respect and courtesy. Mutual commitment combined with mutual respect gives friendship in marriage a chance to grow. Respect develops admiration and esteem. It allows no room for prejudice and sarcasm. A marriage with respect as a core element allows each partner to give and receive affirmation and friendship.

Mutual interests. When a friendship begins early in the relationship and is marked by commitment and respect, it can be further strengthened by areas of activities that both enjoy. Marriage partners who find areas of mutual enjoyment and interests give their relationship extra impetus for developing friendship.

When we speak of mutual interests, we don't mean interests in the children, church activities, house maintenance, and work schedules. Those are not activities which two people enjoy together as friends. We have observed that couples with strong relationships have enjoyable mutual interests such as walking together, traveling, gourmet cooking, photography and picture collecting, mountain climbing, reading aloud and discussing books, furniture making, gardening, sports, social outreaches, or writing.

As the friendship increases, there should be a growing desire to be together—whether doing things or just enjoying each other's company.

Good communication. Common, enjoyable activities need communication to bring the marriage friendship to full flower. And between husband and wife, communication should move to communion. Communion includes the exchange of ideas and thoughts and the sharing of feelings and emotions.

So much has been written and spoken recently about the need for good communication in marriage that the words have begun to assume an obligatory sound. But no set of rules will guarantee good communication. Friendship will do more to stimulate it than technique.

Communication is the need both to speak and to be heard. Sometimes people who have been married for a long time tend not to bother with conversation because they think they know what their partner is going to say. But we must never assume that our spouse has nothing new to say. We all change in outlook and thinking, and our conversations should reflect that.

If you spend much of your time together watching television, turn it off for a couple of evenings and test your capacity to talk. The silence may be deafening! It will force better communication. Your conversational interests should increase with your years of marriage. The desire for good communion grows in direct proportion to the love relationship and to the experience of good past conversations.

Mary and I have grown to really enjoy talking with each other. Of course, we experience times when conflict, busyness, or fatigue make it harder. But when we have not "just talked" for several days, both of us feel the strain and deprivation. Mary is my best critic. She helps me sift ideas. She makes me laugh. We help each other as we talk through the issues of helping our children mature and grow. And we don't always agree on how that should be done! We have found that writing together has given us extra communication in a more neutral setting, where even a good argument is helpful.

Keeping confidences. In any friendship, and most particularly the marriage relationship, keeping confidences shared in times of intimate conversation is crucial to preserving the integrity of that friendship. A husband needs to know he can trust his wife implicitly, and a wife needs to know that when any emotion or secret is shared, it will never pass beyond the confines of their relationship without her express permission. Discretion with confidences is vital to the marriage relationship. Regaining trust takes so much time that it isn't worth a momentary verbal indiscretion with privileged information. "Discretion will protect you, and understanding will guard you" (Proverbs 2:11). "Like a gold ring in a pig's snout is a beautiful woman who shows no discretion" (Proverbs 11:22). "A prudent man keeps his knowledge to himself, but the heart of fools blurts out folly" (Proverbs 12:23).

Encouraging personal goals. In any friendship, it is helpful to know the goals and aspirations of the other person and to contribute to their fulfillment in whatever way possible. This supportive role is doubly necessary in the marriage friendship. You may have mutual goals for your marriage and home, but each partner should have individual goals for personal growth and development. If you know what they are you can help support and encourage your spouse in reaching them.

Jerry and I married before his senior year in college. I really enjoyed my studies and wanted to finish my degree, but four children and seven moves intervened before that was possible. I began taking night courses one at a time. Although we were in the midst of a ministry to cadets at the Air Force Academy and a heavy work schedule for Jerry, I scheduled the classes so Jerry cared for the children whenever possible. When our fourth child, Kristin, was born, I was in the midst of a Shakespeare course. Jerry went to the class in my place, and even participated in the discussions! Finishing college was important to me and after several years of plugging away I got the degree. Jerry's loving support was very important to me through that time.

As I reflect on this time in our lives, I think it was a turning point in our friendship. Up to this point, I had focused on my career, my goals, my education, my ministry—all of which Mary supported beautifully. I encouraged her to pursue finishing college. In retrospect, I don't think I fully understood how important it was to her at the time. But as I supported Mary in one of her goals, our friendship and understanding deepened.

As strange as it may seem, we grew into a more intellectually equal relationship. Prior to that time I think I held her down in her personal growth. This experience helped us recognize each other as completely equal before God and in our communication as husband and wife. We still believe fully in the biblical love and submission relationship of Ephesians 5. But submission and subservience differ greatly. We are equal friends.

How to Build or Improve Friendship with Your Spouse

Now that you know what can get in the way of a friendship with your spouse, and what you need as a basis for that relationship, consider the following practical suggestions for building up a weak marriage friendship or improving an already satisfactory one:

- Review the past privately. Openly discuss problems without defensiveness and criticism. Listen carefully so you can learn about yourself and your spouse. If necessary, discuss problems and issues that have stifled friendship in the past.
- Set aside time to talk. Maybe you can do that twice daily or for longer periods twice weekly, but don't let many days go by without enjoying a free flow of conversation.

- Renew your lifetime commitment to each other.
- Begin doing fun things together. Select one activity you both enjoy and can anticipate with pleasure.
- Individually consider ways you can help your spouse reach his or her personal goals.
- By yourself, pray daily for your marriage partner. We have been saddened to learn that in many Christian marriages, there is little or no prayer for the other partner.
- Together, read the Bible and pray daily. This one factor can strengthen and reinforce your marriage.
- Guard against divisive influences, such as too many unilateral decisions, excluding your spouse from most activities, and differing spiritual commitments. Also guard against complacency in the form of selfishness, an overly materialistic outlook on life, and lack of healthy two-way communication.
- Consciously strive to keep the friendship fresh by remaining an interesting person who is enjoyable to be around. Don't allow yourself to stagnate.
- Keep respect and courtesy at the core of the friendship. Refuse to take each other for granted.

It's never too late to improve a marriage friendship. You may be engaged, newly married, or celebrating your silver wedding anniversary. Perhaps your marriage is strained, unhappy, or collapsing. You may feel the pressure of living with a person you thought you knew but who is apparently changing before your eyes. Perhaps your mate really is not the same person you married. (Indeed, we certainly hope not. We are all changing, growing, and maturing, and our friendships must grow too.) Any marriage friendship can be strengthened by one spouse or both. It is a friendship with more complexities than others, and it requires more time and care than others. Husband and wife must come to the marriage eager to sponsor a lasting, growing, supportive friendship.

The apostle Paul's practical definition of love can help us in fostering the best of marriage friendships. By substituting "a friend" for "love" we gain a clearer perspective of the attitudes and behavior that married friends should have.

> A friend is patient, a friend is kind. A friend does not envy, a friend does not boast, a friend is not proud. A friend is not rude, a friend is not self-seeking, a friend is not easily angered, a friend keeps no record of wrongs. A friend does not delight in evil but rejoices with the truth. A friend always protects, always trusts, always hopes, always perseveres. (Adapted from 1 Corinthians 13:4-7)

Paul's timeless suggestions for exhibiting love can help marriage partners emphasize the loving actions that will allow their friendship to flourish and increase.

Summary

1. The greatest hindrances to friendship in marriage are: an excessively physical focus, a lack of intellectual and emotional interaction, taking each other for granted, and unresolved day-to-day conflict.

2. Friendship in marriage is best established with: an early start, lifetime commitment, respect and courtesy, mutual interests, good communication, keeping confidences, and encouraging personal goals.

CHAPTER 9
Family Friends

F AMILIES LAST FOREVER. You may decide to leave
your family, ignore them, and isolate yourself, but
your mother remains your mother, your brother goes on
being your brother, and assorted aunts, uncles, and
cousins continue in those roles forever. You cannot change
history and heritage.

God alone chooses the circumstances of birth and
heritage. He knows our family environment and destined
it from our conception. "For you created my inmost being;
you knit me together in my mother's womb.... All the
days ordained for me were written in your book before one
of them came to be" (Psalm 139:13 and 16).

God doesn't offer us a choice in our family circle. Even
for adoptions, God knows the natural parents and the

ideal adoptive family. And perhaps God maintains a special niche in his loving heart for families with adopted children, for it is the method by which he received us into his family. "For he *chose* us in him before the creation of the world to be holy and blameless in his sight. In love he predestined us to be adopted as his sons through Jesus Christ, in accordance with his pleasure and will" (Ephesians 1:4-5).

But whether by natural birth or adoption, we all find ourselves bound irrevocably to a family, not of our choosing but of God's plan. We cannot change that relationship.

For that very reason, friendship within the family is of vital importance. Family friendships can provide a buffer, a refuge, and a retreat when other friendships fail. Strong friendship within the family provides a solid foundation for broad friendships outside the family.

Too often, however, instead of exhibiting friendship, closeness, and harmony, families are fractured by discord, suspicion, and bitterness. What causes such sad splits? Why can't families bind together in stability and peace? Why should friendship be so difficult to maintain within immediate and extended family units?

The Vulnerability of Family Friendships

Perhaps the fact that families are permanent lends strength to the tendency to allow irritants to grow out of proportion and offenses to assume more importance than they deserve. Perhaps subconsciously, we recognize the lasting quality of family relationships and we take thoughtless liberties, knowing those ties cannot be severed.

John and Harry, middle-aged brothers, lived in a small midwestern town. They each operated a business and after marriage bought houses next door to each other. They attended the same church, and their children were more like brothers and sisters than cousins.

One spring, John approached Harry and asked him to trim some limbs from a large elm tree in Harry's yard. They were shading a vegetable garden that John had mulched and cultivated for several years.

"Well, I don't know, John. Took a lot of years for the tree to get that big. Couldn't you move your garden over in that corner, there? That spot gets a lot of sun."

"Harry," John answered rather testily. "I've gotten this soil to a perfect condition for vegetables. I'm not going to move the garden now. A few limbs off that elm won't kill it."

"Now look, John. I like this tree. Martha likes to sit under it for picnics. The kids all climb in it. I'm not taking a saw to this tree."

"Well, blast it, Harry! This is stupid! What are a few tree limbs?"

"Don't call me stupid, John," Harry said in a warning tone.

John glared at his brother for a long moment, tightened his jaw, and turned away. The brothers did not speak again for two years. The tree limbs remained in place and John doggedly continued to garden in the shaded plot, occasionally reaching up and slamming his hoe in frustration against the limbs.

Their wives remained friends but spoke only during the daytime when the brothers were away at work. They sorrowed over the break but couldn't penetrate the stubborn resistance of either man. Church members noticed the tension, and townspeople were perplexed by the animosity between the two brothers, once so friendly and agreeable.

Two years later, John's wife called Harry late one evening. "Harry, this is Joan. The doctor told John today that he has cancer. John wanted me to let you know."

A minute later Harry walked through the back door of John's house with tears running down his cheeks. He found John sitting at the table, his head in his hands. John looked up as Harry entered, rose and embraced his brother.

"Forgive me, John," Harry said in a low tone.

"God forgive us both, Harry."

The next morning, shortly after dawn, Harry climbed into the elm tree and began furiously slicing at the overhanging limbs with a chain saw.

John endured several months of disagreeable cancer treatment and experienced an apparent cure. Harry visited him nearly every day he was hospitalized and operated John's business as well as his own.

A happy ending, you say. Yes, but John and Harry both experience deep regrets that they lost two years of friendship. Neither will discuss the cause of the break. They are determined to forget the fracture and want to remember only the healing.

How to Take Care of Family Friendships

The importance of family friendships and the value of their contribution to our lives should make us willing to consider ways to keep these friendships solid, harmonious, and lasting.

Here are some specific suggestions:

- Recognize the inescapable permanence of the family relationships.
- Value family friendships for the lifelong benefit they can bring.
- Be a loyal family friend, not just a relative.

- Double efforts to overlook slights, offenses, and thoughtless remarks.
- Forgive and forget past mistakes and sins.
- Allow relatives to grow and change.
- Refrain from offering unsolicited advice.
- Be quick to sincerely compliment, commend, and approve.
- Avoid comparisons between your achievements, their achievements, or your children's achievements. Resist the temptation to verbally compare one member of the family with another.
- Maintain friendship by any available means when you are separated—letter, phone, small gifts, quick visits.
- Don't presume, without considerable thought and real need, upon family friendship for money, time, or special favors.

In all of your interaction with family members, keep this principle in mind:

> Handle family friendships with particular care, for history is hard to erase and families last forever.

Perhaps these suggestions will give you ideas for considering specific ways to foster and encourage your own family friendships. The value of these friendships cannot be overrated. The deeper your family friendships, the more secure and confident you will be in all other relationships.

When I was a girl, I remember attending many family functions with my parents. My father had thirteen brothers and sisters, many of whom still lived in the same general area, so family gatherings assumed large proportions. My memories of those times abound with sounds of hearty laughter, endless conversation interspersed with Norwegian phrases, intermingled with more laughter and frequent reminiscences. There must have been times of friction and tension, but as a child observer, I didn't see them.

These many experiences demonstrated the joy of a friendly family to me. Besides those group friendships, I also saw intimate friendships within that large circle—brother with brother, sister with sister, in-law with in-law, and cousin with cousin.

And now I see members of the older generation befriending not only the second but the third generation as well.

Biblical Examples

Christian families possess the greatest potential for strong friendships because they have biblical teaching and examples both to warn them and to encourage them.

The Scriptures are filled with plenty of negative examples where friendships never formed, or split as a result of anger, quarreling, jealousy, or hatred. These bitter family splits provide illustrations that can prevent us from following the same destructive pattern.

Early in the history of man, Cain killed his brother Abel in a fit of jealous rage over God's approval of Abel's sacrifice.

Jacob and Esau split their friendship and their families as a result of Jacob's scheming selfishness and Esau's momentary weakness. Although they were reunited, the bitterness between the descendants of these brothers flames the tensions in the Middle East even today.

Rachel and Leah, two beautiful sisters who were both married to Jacob, seethed with resentment and jealousy toward each other when they should have formed a fast friendship to buffer their exile in a strange land.

Joseph's brothers reached a point of killing rage in frustration with parental favoritism.

In King David's complicated family, hatred, incest, and murder dominated the relationships of the children. Amnon defiled his sister. In a chilling retaliation Absalom ordered the slaughter of his brother. Later, Solomon and another brother Adonijah exchanged hostility over the succession to the throne and Adonijah ultimately was assassinated. Dreadful occurrences, all, for a family that should have been bound by love and supportive good will.

The Bible also records positive examples of families, however, which demonstrate the friendships that God intends for the obedient Christian family.

Ruth, Orpah, and Naomi provide a beautiful example of family friendships that span the age gap and the in-law hurdle.

Esther and Mordecai demonstrate the beneficial and protective aspects of family friendship.

Peter and Andrew reveal the spiritual value of brotherly friendship. The eagerness with which Andrew led Peter to meet Jesus shows the spiritual concern of one brother for another.

Timothy's mother and grandmother, Eunice and Lois, must have enjoyed a warm friendship as they worked together to give Timothy a sound Christian atmosphere in a household that included a pagan husband and father.

Loving relationships are clearly taught in the Bible. For Christian people, the first attempts at friendship should be within the family. God has placed us in close proximity with family members, in part to practice the art of friendship and enjoy the advantages of those close friendships.

Family Subgroups

Special subgroups within the family provide natural settings for friendship development. For clarification we will refer to the immediate family as parents, children, brothers, and sisters, and to the extended family as aunts, uncles, cousins, in-laws, and grandparents.

Individual families may restructure these classifications if, for instance, grandparents or an aunt or uncle live with the immediate family. Intimate friendships are most natural in the immediate family, but will certainly develop in the extended family as well.

Family members enjoy distinct advantages in making friends with one another because so much groundwork has been laid. No preliminary discussions are needed regarding family background or personal history—sometimes not even regarding motivations, ambitions, fears, and hopes. So much of a friendship depends on explanations of these aspects. But in a family group, this understanding is readily available because of long acquaintance.

A look at some of the subgroups can help us understand lasting and rewarding friendship in the family. Perhaps you feel satisfied with your family relationships at this point in time. You may have a relaxed and amiable atmosphere in your family group. If so, these next sections may help you deepen those friendships or prevent friction and discord in the future.

You may, however, be a person who feels alienated and estranged from your family group. That is a dreadful experience, even temporarily. These sections may help you discover the source of the problem and ways to restore the relationship to a healthy friendship.

Parents. God considered this relationship so impor-

tant that he established it as one of the ten command-
ments. "Honor your father and your mother, so that you
may live long in the land the Lord your God is giving you"
(Exodus 20:12).

The apostle Paul emphasized this principle again
when he wrote to the Christians at Ephesus. " 'Honor your
father and mother'—which is the first commandment with
a promise—'that it may go well with you and that you may
enjoy long life on the earth' " (Ephesians 6:2-3).

Does honor mean friendship? No, but it provides a
secure basis for friendship. To honor means to respect and
esteem.

But what if you don't respect your parents? Some
people feel nothing but contempt and anger toward their
parents for real or imagined wrongs.

A Christian who nurtures such feelings should seek
forgiveness and cleansing, because he is disobeying God.
God's word is clear—"Honor your parents." God does not
include any qualifying statements such as "if they're nice
people," "if they have provided for you well," or "if they
keep out of your affairs." God says, "Honor."

Lila Trotman, widow of Navigators founder Dawson
Trotman, said in a message, "If you can't honor your
parents for anything else, you can honor them because
God chose them to give you life." This is a good beginning
for the respect and esteem necessary as a basis for
friendship with parents.

We often find it difficult to be sincere friends with our
parents because we expect them to be ideal—never
hurting us, always loving perfectly, never failing.
Common sense reveals the impossibility of such a
demand, but tucked away in our inner being, we wish for
such people as parents.

Recognizing and accepting the flaws of other people,

especially close family members, takes us a giant leap forward in the process of personal maturity. Friendship with parents will have to wait until we can overlook their imperfections, forgive past mistakes, and accept them just as they are, still in life's process of maturing, or just plain human.

One woman told us, "I don't remember ever thinking of my mother as a person when I was growing up—a person, that is, with a personality, likes and dislikes and feelings. She was just Mama."

But, of course, parents are people with all of the complexities of any personality. Any friendship begins with a knowledge and understanding of the other person. How well do you know your parents? What are their likes and dislikes? What activities do they enjoy? What do they fear? What are their hopes and ambitions? What types of people do they enjoy being with? What makes them laugh or cry?

If you feel your friendship is weak, spend some time thinking about your parents as people. Then consider ways you could encourage or strengthen a friendship with them.

- What contribution can you make to their enjoyment of life?
- What can you refrain from doing that would please them?
- Have you complimented them lately?
- When did you last express love for them?
- Have you had fun together lately?
- Can you think of an enjoyable activity to do together?
- Have you ever sacrificed time, money, effort, or personal plans on their behalf?

One of the highlights of our adult life has been our

growing friendship with our parents. Don't deny yourself and your parents the pleasure of friendship. If wounded feelings and harsh words have characterized your relationship in the past, resolve to ask for forgiveness and work toward a friendship that will be enriching and satisfying for them and for you. Incorporate this principle into your attitudes and your actions:

> Parents are a special trust and responsibility from the Lord. Guard their friendship.

Even if your parents are not Christians, the Bible makes no distinction. Your responsibility to them remains the same. By your loving concern you may lead them to Christ. They can be great friends, and through that friendship see Christ in you.

One of our dear friends in England, Heather Rogerson, led her eighty-year-old father to the Lord shortly before he died. He had resisted spiritual matters throughout his life, but through Heather's patient, loving, and consistent witness, he came to the Lord. Perhaps God will grant you the same privilege.

Brothers and sisters. Adult siblings must recognize that as brothers and sisters mature and marry and move, they become different people than they were in the parental home. It is important that each person be given room for change and that he relate to others accordingly. Learning to know, understand, and enjoy that new person is part of the fun of friendship within a family.

Perhaps your relationship with brothers and sisters has broken or been weakened by neglect and indifference. You may have observed others enjoying close family ties, and would like some of the same yourself. How do you go about that?

Use the principles in chapters four and five on

initiating and maintaining friendships, or, if you've had a breach at some point, start the healing process with the restoration steps outlined in chapter seven. Remember that family friendships require special care.

Once you have built a close friendship with a brother or sister, you will grow to treasure it so much that you will carefully guard it against the destroying effects of criticism, hostility, and indifference.

Although most breaches between siblings occur in adulthood, friendships between brothers and sisters can be encouraged while they are still children and living together within the family.

Any parents who observe their children squabbling— from the frustrated squabbling of toddlers where vocabulary fails and fat little fists beat on chubby bodies, to the stinging, cutting verbal barbs of one teenaged sibling to another—may despair of ever seeing friendship between them, yet out of all this sibling conflict can grow some of the deepest friendships of a lifetime.

If you're a parent, use the following tips to help promote friendship between your children.

- Try to commend and praise your children as often as possible. Avoid excessive criticism. Friendship fails to flourish in a negative atmosphere.
- Never, never compare one child to another. It makes a no-win situation and pits one child in anger against another.
- Create activities that place children in proximity and require cooperation—work projects, discussions, crafts, sports events. Keep the tone positive. If bickering starts, call a halt to the fun.
- Pray daily for friendship between your children.
- Let your children observe your friendship with your own brothers and sisters.

I have two brothers and two sisters. All of us are in, or approaching, middle age. I recall a significant quantity of bickering in our childhood (our father can probably recall a good deal more than I can), but those early skirmishes haven't prevented close ties today. We were given a strong Christian heritage and an example of friendly parents, which probably influenced our relationships today.

We enjoy being together, jogging in a large group, eating favorite childhood foods, and reminiscing about the past. Although there are four of us scattered widely over the western half of the United States with the fifth sister in east Africa, we manage to be together quite often. We fill the interludes with phone calls and letters.

Within this friendly circle of five are two sets of smaller and more intense friendships among the sisters and between the brothers. Part of the reason these relationships continue to thrive is that those who have married into our family have harmonized well with the existing family friendships, a key factor in the satisfying friendships of brothers and sisters.—(Mary)

Unless in-laws tolerate, even encourage, the established friendships, those friendships will suffer strain and eventually fail. A brother–sister friendship cannot survive under the attack of a hostile spouse.

It doesn't matter if you are twenty-one or eighty-one; a happy friendship with a brother or sister will enhance your life. If such a relationship does not now exist for you, consider means by which you can establish and foster such a friendship.

Children. Renee and her mother shop together at least once a month. They start early in the morning after Renee has placed her children in school. They enjoy a long, leisurely lunch and sometimes an afternoon play. Every Sunday they teach the nursery department of the Sunday school together.

John and his son Chip set aside one week each year from their jobs for fishing. They shrug into backpacks loaded with sleeping bags, fishing gear, and food and hike a torturously long way into the mountains where they claim the fishing is unsurpassed, and, better yet, no one else is around.

Myrtle visits each of her daughters once a year for two weeks. Each daughter pleads with Myrtle to stay longer, but at the end of two weeks of fun and visiting and laughter, she hugs them warmly, climbs on a plane, and goes home.

Dan entered his father's law firm after college. Although they work together every day, often after the secretaries leave the office for the day, Dan and his father brew another pot of coffee in the client's waiting room, loosen their ties, and talk for an hour before heading home.

What do all of these people have in common? They are more than parents and children. They have moved to an expanded dimension of adult friendship.

Dr. Joe Aldrich, President of Multnomah School of the Bible, stresses in his seminar on child raising that parents must move from a point of correction to a point of counsel with their children. And, we think he would agree, as the child strikes out on his own, parents must move beyond the point of counsel to the fullest extent of the relationship—friendship.

A parent trying to control a twenty-five-year-old son appears ludicrous indeed. And a thirty-year-old daughter needing mothering is a pathetic version of maturity. The ultimate success in parenting allows us to interact with our grown children as mature, capable Christian people who can now be our friends. Ideally, the friendship has been building since the child was an infant, but in adulthood, counsel and correction must be replaced by friendship in order to have a satisfying relationship.

If you are a parent, there are several things you can do to make this transition from counseled child to mature friend possible.

- Be willing to release your children from your directive care. Friendships never mature when one person perpetually governs the other.
- Take a genuine interest in the affairs and viewpoints of your children.
- Recall only positive memories from the past and set the tone for your children to do the same.
- Offer advice and counsel *only* when asked, except if you see your child entering into sin. Then this principle of Scripture applies: "Brothers, if someone is caught in a sin, you who are spiritual should restore him gently" (Galatians 6:1).
- Even if you have previously been a nosey, interfering parent, resolve to change. But do allow your child time to realize the emergence of a new you. Allow time for your previously marred relationship to build into friendship.
- Pray faithfully for a lasting, rewarding friendship with your grown children *and* their families.

Extended family (aunts, uncles, grandparents, cousins). A photograph from a recent family reunion shows Aunt Isabel seated at a picnic surrounded by nieces and nephews. Her white hair shows plainly among the dark and blond heads pressed close to hers. They are all looking at the sketch pad in her lap, evidently getting a quick art lesson, for Aunt Isabel is the family artist.

But more than that, she typifies the ideal extended family member, for she relates well to her own generation and finds the younger generation interesting and worthy of her time and friendship. She maintains an interest in ideas and events and people. She converses easily on a wide range of subjects. Approaching eighty, she finds fulfillment in teaching art classes for residents of a nearby rest home. It is a pleasure to be her friend.

I called our college-age son in Colorado recently to see if he wanted us to arrange transportation for him to come home at Christmas time.

"Well, Dad, I'm not sure yet. I've saved some money and I thought I might go to Iowa. Just wait a few weeks and I'll let you know."

The only person in Iowa Steve knows well, knows at all for that matter, is his great-grandmother. What draws a twenty-two-year-old man to visit his great-grandmother, well into her late eighties? Friendship.

The separation of years falls away as they extend love and companionship to each other. They talk of old times and new, go out for pizza, watch television together, and drive around to visit Grandma's friends. Grandma flexes her schedule for Steve and he slows his long-legged pace to match hers.

When our daughter Karen heard of Steve's planned visit to Iowa, she decided to use her "puppy money" (from selling a recent litter of springer spaniel puppies) to fly to Denver and go with Steve to see Grandma. In spite of a raging blizzard and car trouble, they made it to Iowa and thoroughly enjoyed the time with Great-Grandma.

Within the extended family you will probably be able to maintain several close friends, many casual friends, and perhaps an intimate friend. Certainly all family members should be friends at some level.

Unfortunately, many families number some enemies among their relatives. How very sad, especially when disputes and hostilities characterize the interactions of a Christian family. We need to allow God to direct those relationships as we assume the role of peacemaker and rebuild wounded ties.

Take advantage of your extended family to give you a sense of family history and spiritual heritage. Grandparents, aunts, and uncles can do a great deal to enlarge your understanding of family history and, if your ancestors were Christians, to increase your faith as you hear of God's faithfulness to your forebearers.

Assume a responsibility for the salvation of your family. Live the Christian life before them, extending the gospel in love and concern when the opportunity arises. You may be the only one in your family who knows and shares Christ. What a privilege to give family friendships the new dimension of Christ as a linking bond.

Allow your children to see your friendships with aunts, uncles, and cousins, and draw them into such friendships. Appreciate the family in which God has placed you. Resolve to promote harmony and friendship.

Nearly twenty-five years ago, I met Jerry's mother. She knew we were considering marriage while still in college, but she gave no negative advice or hint of disapproval. On a blistering hot summer day she welcomed me into her home for the first time. In a natural, hospitable way, she made me feel at ease.

She maintained that atmosphere of warmth and acceptance throughout our long friendship. Over the years there must have been incidents she noticed that

*troubled her—perhaps the way I raised her
grandchildren, responded to her son, failed to write
frequently enough, or whatever. But I cannot remember
one time when she criticized or corrected me. I do
remember many times when she complimented me,
commented on some small achievement, or thanked me
for something.*

*Could I have asked for more in a mother-in-law? I
know she wasn't a perfect woman. I just happen to
think she was a perfect mother-in-law.*

In-laws. Rare indeed is the person without in-laws. If
marriage doesn't quickly plunge us into the world of in-
laws, our brothers or sisters bring them to us. Harmonious
relationships require a warm, friendly assimilation of in-
laws into an existing family.

If any word should characterize the treatment, as well
as the behavior, of in-laws, it is *tolerance*—then more
tolerance—and still *more* tolerance. In-laws aren't wrong,
just different. Backgrounds vary, experiences differ,
personal preferences diverge. But they need not split a
relationship. With tolerance and time, in-laws can add a
fresh dimension to a family as friends and relatives.

Dwell on the positive aspects of your in-law family.
Withhold comparisons and criticism. Allow time for
acceptance and for friendships to develop. Enjoy your role
as an in-law and anticipate warm friendships with the in-
laws that enter your family.

No matter how many special subgroups are involved,
families provide the most natural setting for fostering
friendships. Delight in the friendships your family has
already provided. Resolve to keep them strong and whole.
Expect and work toward new and deeper friendships. You
will be richer for it.

Summary

1. To take special care of family friendships, use the following suggestions:

Recognize the inescapable permanence of family relationships.

Value family friendships for their lifelong potential.

Resolve to be a loyal family friend.

Double efforts to overlook offenses.

Forgive and forget past mistakes and sins.

Allow relatives to grow and change.

Don't offer advice unless you're asked.

Be quick to compliment, commend, and approve.

Don't make comparisons.

Maintain friendship by any available means.

Don't presume upon family favors, time, or money.

2. Specific family subgroups provide many opportunities for cultivating friendships—with parents, with brothers and sisters, with children, within the extended family, and with in-laws.

Principles

1. Handle family friendships with particular care, for history is hard to erase and families last forever.

2. Parents are a special trust and responsibility from the Lord. Guard their friendship.

CHAPTER 10

Friendships in the Church

AS JOHN AND MARTHA walked into the church they scanned the crowd. When they spotted the Larsons they carefully went the other way, avoiding any contact. The air of tension between them and the Larsons affected not only the four of them but also at least a dozen others who knew what was taking place just then inside the church door. The tragedy of the situation was more profound because of the years of friendship between these couples. But because of a few minor disagreements over the last few months, the fiber of their friendship rotted away. Soon one couple would probably leave the fellowship of the church.

David Martin stood in the same milieu of people completely oblivious to the tension, not knowing either of the couples. He shifted about nervously as people seemed to politely ignore this bearded young man in jeans and turtleneck shirt. His contrast to the church uniform of the day was obvious. Then his eyes lit up and he relaxed as Rich came careening down the corridor toward him. "Hi, Dave. Sorry to be late. Let's go over here and meet some of my other friends."

About twenty feet away, Mike and Kathy Hagen struck up a conversation with a couple about their age. On the way to church they had discussed trying to develop a relationship with the other couple, since they thought they would get along well. But as they talked, the other couple kept impatiently looking over the crowd, tossing out greetings to people they knew. They responded only minimally to Mike and Kathy. It was apparent that this relationship would not click. As the couples parted, Mike shrugged his shoulders and Kathy felt disappointed.

Others gathered in small circles of animated conversation. But most went silently about the business of getting from door to pew with hardly a word—and slipped out the same way.

The church is the body of Christ—the fellowship of believers. It is the place where intimate friendships should spawn and grow. Yet it is a place that often houses strangers—or so it seems to many who enter expecting a different world than the office, factory, or neighborhood. Many people do not find the friendships they seek and need in the church. The church *should* be one of the key seedbeds for deep friendships. What hinders the local church from functioning as an ideal catalyst to friendships? Certainly herculean efforts are being made to mold the church into a caring community—church growth experiments, house churches, growth groups, and many other innovative changes. But why are they needed?

The Dilemma of Church Friendships

The local church faces attacks from many quarters. It seems that everybody in some way demands that the church meet his own expectations. No matter what a church does, it will draw criticism. It cannot please everyone.

But aside from differing expectations, there are some real dilemmas that a caring church faces as it attempts to develop a friendship-oriented fellowship. What are the barriers that the church is up against as it tries to meet people's needs? We see six specific issues or dilemmas.

1. *There is no longer a survival necessity for interdependence within the local church.* Until fifty years ago society was largely rural and neighborhood oriented. People had to depend upon each other in both the community and the church. Today we live in a world of exploding computerized technology and an increasing dependence on government as protector and provider. When trouble strikes, people call professionals—doctors, lawyers, plumbers, mechanics, or social agencies. It is not wrong to call these experts, but it does erode our dependence on each other. Even within the church we depend on secular systems such as insurance, unemployment compensation, or Medicare to meet or supplement immediate needs. Consequently, caring friendships are not so easily spawned.

2. *True neighborhoods today are either few or none.* Consequently, the neighborhood church has virtually died. Many people do not even know the names of their neighbors. People come and go unnoticed and uncared for. There is little sharing of common interests or concern for the common good. And many people in church do not live within easy distance of one another. In fact, churches may

be the only area of common contact through the week. Church members often live and work in separate worlds. Thus it takes considerable effort to become friends because of the extra personal time necessary to develop a friendship.

3. *The automobile has changed the nature of the church* as much as any other single technological event. This problem is even more pronounced than the lack of true neighborhood contact and interaction. People are no longer restricted to horse-drawn carriages or walking distance to get to church. Now they get in the car and drive many miles to a church where no one else may even come from their part of town. If they don't like the church, they can add ten minutes to their driving time and go to another. We know people who drive sixty miles to another city to attend church.

This mobility was strongly impressed on our minds as we observed our daughter coming home on a weekend from college, twenty-five miles away. She borrowed the car to drive back to the church she attends to go to Sunday school. A one way trip is forty-five minutes! Even twenty years ago that would have been unthinkable.

The automobile has paved the way for very large churches. This is not necessarily a negative factor, since many of these large churches have great ministries. But it does deeply affect the building of friendships because the congregation is scattered. In a metropolitan church it would not be uncommon to meet a person you like and find that you live an hour's driving distance apart.

4. *The church is a melting pot of people.* It draws together men and women from every social and cultural background. They differ in secular profession, social status, financial income, race, family background, spiritual growth, age, family makeup, and cultural

heritage. In our idealistic view of the body of Christ, we believe that laborer and doctor, educated and uneducated ought to relate harmoniously in fellowship. And they can and do. But seldom do they become close friends. In deeper relationships the church often segments and divides. People seek out those with common backgrounds or interests. Crossing cultural lines is not easy. This great diversity, though positive in the concept of the church, militates against an easy development of friendships. Real frustration can set in when a person feels guilty about not developing relationships with many and focusing on a few who share common interests or age. But that is the reality of church today.

5. *Conflicts often arise over petty issues.* In almost every church some level of conflict usually exists. And the longer a person is in a church, the more likely that some conflict will strike him personally. Conflict itself is not bad if it is handled properly. But issues such as music, youth programs, nursery schedules, social functions, purchase of new carpet, or repainting the hallways typify sources of petty conflicts. Soon these chip away at the fabric of friendships. Gossip spreads the infection and people polarize, often not even knowing why. These conflicts over unimportant issues disturb the spirit of relationships like static on a radio broadcast. Soon people turn it off and back away from the fellowship.

6. Finally, *the church has been weakened as the primary source of spiritual input for Christians today.* Television, radio, and parachurch groups provide a menu of spiritual feeding that often overshadows the church. Though most of these influences intend to supplement, not replace, the church, they do decrease people's dependence on the church. And most people will develop their relationships where they receive primary spiritual help.

Although each of these six issues exerts both positive and negative influences, all of them generally affect friendship building in the church in a negative manner. All of them force the church to work harder to create an environment conducive to spiritual growth. And they must be considered when thinking of fostering better friendships in the church body.

To keep our perspective in balance, we would not advocate anyone developing *all* their intimate or close friendships within the church. That would be too self-centered, and would greatly hinder relationships outward into the community. To prevent narrowness and isolation, we should develop friendships outside as well as inside the church body. But before we take a look at how churches can combat the dilemmas above by taking specific and practical steps to foster friendships, let's establish some practical realities of church friendships to prevent unrealistic expectations.

A Realistic View

We each dream of the perfect local church that precisely meets *our* every expectation. But as the saying goes, "If you find the perfect church, don't join it because it won't be perfect anymore." No church is perfect. No person is perfect. Our human frailties foul us up at every turn. And, of course, we imperfect humans make up the local church. Although the ideal fellowship still persists in our minds, we must live in the nitty-gritty world of reality.

As we look at the church, we can identify several things that the church and people in that church cannot do. We live with serious personal and corporate limitations. If we understand some of those limitations, perhaps we can make peace with their reality. After all, who wants to live in a dream world that doesn't exist?

The first of these limitations is the general principle that we established in chapter two, and that is important to keep in mind when considering church friendships:

> Everyone has a *limited* capacity for friendship,
> and each person has a *different* capacity for
> numbers of friendships.

Since each person is limited in the friendships he or she can maintain, not everyone in a church can be friends with everyone else. Neither time nor emotional capacity permit that many relationships.

Accept this reality and be tolerant of others as you pursue friendship in the church. Remember the principle from chapter four about initiating friendships: "Rejection of friendship advances does not equal rejection of the person. Many other factors are involved." Think of your dilemma if you felt obligated to take everyone you met in church into your friendship circle.

A second limitation in ideal church friendships is another important principle, this time directly related to our biblical call to Christlikeness:

> As Christians, we are obligated to extend
> to every person unlimited acceptance *but not*
> unlimited friendship.

The Scriptures clearly teach unlimited acceptance of other Christians. "Accept one another, then, just as Christ accepted you, in order to bring praise to God" (Romans 15:7; see also Romans 14:1). Accept others, no matter how unlovely they may be. Accept them as Christ accepted us—with our faults, our sin, and our many needs. Acceptance means warmly drawing others into the body of Christ with love and friendliness; it does not mean that we must develop friendship with everyone—not even with everyone who wants our friendship. We must make choices according to our limitations, our capacities, and our personal needs.

A third limiting reality of church life is this social principle about how we interact with each other:

> Social groupings and divisions legitimately
> exist in the church.

This does not mean that all social groupings are good, but simply that any large number of people must break down into smaller units for meaningful relationships to exist or develop. When the divisions become exclusive cliques we then exceed the bounds of Scripture.

James clarifies these issues for us by condemning preferential treatment. In chapter two, verses 1-4 of his epistle, he clearly portrays a church response that is *not* one of Christlike acceptance:

> My brothers, as believers in our glorious Lord Jesus
> Christ, don't show favoritism. Suppose a man comes
> into your meeting wearing a gold ring and fine clothes,
> and a poor man in shabby clothes also comes in. If you
> show special attention to the man wearing fine clothes
> and say, "Here's a good seat for you," but say to the
> poor man, "You stand there," or, "Sit on the floor by my
> feet," have you not discriminated among yourselves and
> become judges with evil thoughts?

We must not show preference. But we must relate in smaller units, which practically will be social groupings.

Fourth, we realize that whether we like it or not, we are limited by this principle:

> Problems and conflict will always be
> present in any church body.

Their presence should not discourage us, but a lack of any attempt to solve them should give us grave concern. If we become disenchanted with people or with a church just because there are problems or because we see conflict, we deny one of the cardinal functions of the church—to help people grow through problems and conflict. We are told, "Carry each other's burdens, and in this way you will fulfill the law of Christ" (Galatians 6:2). We are not to avoid contact with those in trouble. Nor should we avoid conflict with someone in the process of developing a friendship. By resolving the conflict, the bonds of friendship will be strengthened. Problems and conflict are facts of life in a church. In fact, they are facts of life wherever there are people. Only a hermit escapes conflict with other people. But a hermit has no friends.

The fifth limitation in church friendships is a principle which may seem obvious, but it is one which we often need to remind ourselves of in order to maintain a realistic view:

> Every person has idealistic expectations both for
> friendship and for church relationships—which
> will never be perfectly met.

When a person or a group fails to meet our mental test of conformity to our expectations, we tend to reject them and close them out of our life. Yet *we* fail to meet others' expectations of us—and even resent the pressure of their expectations.

If we could only realize that we fall short of God's standards for us, and yet he accepts us totally, we might realize that no one will ever meet our expectations perfectly—not even our spouse, nor our children, nor our intimate friends. In fact, we don't even meet our expectations of ourselves. So how can we demand it of

others? We must be realistic in our expectations of the
church body and of individuals when we measure them
against our friendship standards.

A Church that Generates Friendships

After an exciting conference of almost fifteen hundred
people, one person commented that he was surrounded by
people but still very lonely. Crowds of people do not keep a
person from being lonely. No church, just by its numbers,
can dispel loneliness or spawn friendship.

But certainly the church ought to be a hotbed for the
growth of budding friendships. The Scriptures teach that
such relationships in the church ought to be qualitatively
different than relationships in the world.

The apostle Paul desperately needed friends. He
longed for them. He valued them. He took pains to mention
them by name in his epistles. And he was not a man alone.
Paul was surrounded by friends, and he was dependent
upon help from them. In Romans 16 Paul reveals the
network of friends he established.

> I commend to you our sister Phoebe, *a servant of the
> church* in Cenchrea...receive her...for she has been *a
> great help* to many people, including me. (verse 1-2)
> Greet Priscilla and Aquila, *my fellow workers* in
> Christ Jesus. They risked their lives for me. (verses 3–4)
> Greet *my dear friend* Epenetus, who was the first
> convert to Christ in the province of Asia. (verse 5)
> Greet Ampliatus, *whom I love* in the Lord. (verse 8)
> Greet Urbanus, *our fellow worker* in Christ, and *my
> dear friend* Stachys. (verse 9)

Paul's titles for his associates—"servant," "a great
help," "fellow workers," "dear friend"—describe godly
friendships. Throughout his epistles and his teaching on

the local church there is an emphasis on relationships among the brethren. And in Paul's life not only do we see a relationship of brothers and sisters in the family of God, but we also see a relationship of human interdependencies and friendship.

Paul was involved in both evangelism and follow-up, and he developed friends by reaching out with others to make disciples of Jesus Christ. Paul's friends were his fellow workers—brothers and sisters in battle—who risked their lives with him to preach the gospel. From their example, we can establish a principle which governs the characteristics of a church that generates friendships:

> Biblical friendships in the church are developed
> in the midst of spiritual battle.

Thus friendships in the church develop not only in the prayer meetings and preaching services, or in the intimate social activities of small groups of Christians, but also in the midst of concern for the lost. We must constantly fight our innate tendency to huddle together in the seeming safety of closed Christian fellowship. Any fellowship that turns in on itself with no outreach soon infects itself with seeds of discord and is doomed to split and die. A focus that is too inward breeds conflict and forces us to select the wrong enemy to fight against.

True friendships are born and developed in the smoke and heat of the spiritual battle between the forces of Satan and the forces of God. They are nurtured by binding wounds and bearing burdens, and this includes the wounds of the church body as well as the burden of the lost.

The church that desires to be a spawning ground for biblical friendships, then, must be a church that fosters— even demands—a commitment to reach out to the non-

Christian segment of our society, as well as one that encourages and promotes the spiritual growth of its own members. Unless both evangelism and caring for the body are part of the spiritual battle, the fellowship will soon die.

In order to understand this balance between ministry to the body and ministry to unbelievers, it is important to distinguish between friendship and fellowship, and between friendship and being friendly. Understanding these distinctions will help our perspective on what should occur in the church, for the congregation that has these aspects in the right balance will be effective both in building up itself and in reaching out to others.

Fellowship is the spiritual interaction of Christians centered around the word and the person of Jesus Christ. It involves Christians of all backgrounds, ages, and maturity levels, both as a group and individually. It knows no time frame for relationships. Therefore, it can take place even between strangers.

Friendship, on the other hand, is a personal relationship developed between two people over a period of time. Friends experience a deeper level of fellowship because of their friendship.

And we must not confuse friendship with the simple act of being friendly. We should be friendly to everyone in the church, but we can be friends with only a limited number of people. Friendliness is an action. Friendship is a continuing relationship.

Although fellowship can take place with strangers, can true fellowship *continue* in a church where friendships do not exist? We believe not. Christian fellowship revolves not around activities, but around relationships. Specifically, these relationships are:

1. Our individual relationship to Christ. "We proclaim to you what we have seen and heard, so that you also may

have fellowship with us. And our fellowship is with the Father and with his Son, Jesus Christ" (1 John 1:3).

2. Our joint (corporate) relationship with Christ. "But if we walk in the light, as he is in the light, we have fellowship with one another, and the blood of Jesus, his Son, purifies us from every sin" (1 John 1:7).

3. Our relationships to one another. "And let us consider how we may spur one another on toward love and good deeds. Let us not give up meeting together, as some are in the habit of doing, but let us encourage one another—and all the more as you see the Day approaching" (Hebrews 10:24-25).

When friendships permeate a church fellowship, a new level of corporate worship is experienced. A new freedom of public sharing develops. A warmth of relationships sends out a distinct aroma even to a stranger. And when the friendships are balanced with outward friendliness, the stranger is drawn into the fellowship and made to feel a part, rather than an intruder. We need this kind of church fellowship.

Now that we've examined the dilemmas which the church is up against as it tries to foster friendships, reviewed some pragmatic principles that must be taken into account in any realistic view of friendship within the church, and established the basic principle which characterizes a friendship-generating church, let's examine some practical steps that the local church can take in order to stimulate the growth and development of friendship within its congregation as well as with visitors.

Develop small groups. Make sure that the church has many opportunities for contact in small units, such as home Bible studies, Sunday school classes, periodic seminars, small prayer fellowships, planned social events with small numbers, men's or women's events, retreats, discipleship programs, choirs, work projects, and dozens of other activities. People need small groups to get acquainted with each other, and the church must provide the opportunity.

Teach and practice friendship. Establish a spirit of friendliness among church leadership and church regulars. Use whatever means possible to greet visitors, to remember people's names (some churches use name tags), and to talk briefly with many. Friendliness costs so little. Lack of it costs a lot—it marks a church as cold and indifferent. This is often a problem that occurs with growth, but with effort it can be overcome.

Encourage homogenous functions. Identify and encourage functions of the church that focus on specific segments of the body. We tend to make every function or meeting of the church open to anyone, yet specialized and even "by-invitation" functions will draw people in a way that general meetings will not. Many people simply will not open up in a broad mixed group. When they get in a small homogeneous group they will often share, ask questions, and interact openly. Consider groups of singles, young couples, retired people, working women, executives, widows, divorced men and women, and so forth.

We must not be afraid to be both selective and exclusive in church activities. In these segmented, homogeneous groups, friendships have a greater likelihood of developing. Think of friendship as a particular variety of seed which requires a certain kind of soil and a certain kind of care to grow. Without the right conditions, friendship doesn't even sprout, much less bear fruit.

Teach and encourage hospitality. Place a stronger emphasis on hospitality in the church. Teach the meaning of biblical hospitality, which is not the same as entertaining. They overlap, but are significantly different.

Romans 12:13 commands us, "Share with God's people who are in need. Practice hospitality." The biblical concept of hospitality differs greatly from entertainment. When we entertain we plan ahead, invite those we want, clean house, buy food, prepare a meal, and finally welcome the people to our home and table.

The New Testament definition of hospitality, on the other hand, pictures a Christian family fleeing the persecutions of Rome, walking into a town, seeking out a Christian family, appearing at their door unannounced, and being welcomed and cared for as family. Since most friendships develop in the context of some small group, someone must initiate the groups and provide the place. As individuals in a congregation practice hospitality in their homes they may find personal friends or provide the setting for others to become friends.

Some Christians possess the gift of hospitality. For most it must be learned. All Christians have received the command. By providing specific teaching and motivation on hospitality, the church can create many more seed plots for initiating and developing friendships.

Teach and practice conflict resolution. Christians must learn how to resolve conflicts biblically to be successful in developing biblical friendships. The church should set the pattern for conflict resolution in both teaching and practice. Only the leaders and staff can do this. If they do not resolve conflicts successfully, they will never succeed in teaching or influencing the congregation to do so.

Friendship will either be strengthened or broken by conflict. Ignored and unresolved conflict breaks friendship; recognized and resolved conflict builds friendship. (See chapter seven for a more detailed discussion of conflict resolution.)

Stimulate biblical fellowship. By this we mean the kind of fellowship discussed earlier, as described in Hebrews 10:24-25. One crucial aspect of this fellowship is learning to share needs and concerns. As people see the reality of a Christlike life and the honesty of sharing, they will share in return. A deeper relationship will develop, which may lead to friendship.

A final reality of friendship in the church cries out for recognition. Most new Christians and non-Christians do not come to church because they like it or because they realize their need of it. They come because a friend brings them. In an increasingly secular society, fewer and fewer people possess roots in any church. The idea of going is foreign to them. When they do go, they don't have any sentimental memories to fall back on to help them accept or enjoy a worship service. They do not automatically feel emotionally or spiritually satisfied.

But as they come with a friend, that friend guides them to other people and eases the unfamiliarity of the new activity. They come together, introduced to Christian worship by the friend's care and example. Thus friendship plays a crucial role in church growth:

New Christians are drawn into the fellowship by friends.

At this point you may be asking, "What can I do as a church member to help spawn friendships?" A few very simple actions can go a long way. We suggest you try some of these:

- Be friendly yourself.
- Apply the principles of friendship taught earlier in the book, especially in chapters four and five.
- Learn to extend yourself to others in hospitality.
- Develop friends, but avoid cliques.
- Be part of some small group effort in your church.

Pastors—A Special Case

A small group of pastors and their wives gathered for a seminar on friendships and relationships. As we presented some of the material from this book, several of the seminar participants responded with heartfelt emotion to our discussion of their special need for friendship. Afterwards one wife came with tears in her eyes and said, "We have been in our church for seven years and I don't have one friend." This illustrates a fundamental principle:

Pastors and their wives need personal friends.

It seems like a simple statement of the obvious. Yet in practice the pastor and his wife tend to become isolated. They often find it difficult to develop friendships in their own congregation. Doesn't it seem incongruous that everyone but the pastor should find his deepest friendships in the body? Often, the only people a couple in the ministry can share intimately with are another pastoral couple. And usually they are not geographically close. Some meet their need in a multiple-staff church, but even there the chemistry of the relationship is not always conducive to a Level Three friendship.

Remember that a pastor is a real person. He is flesh and blood like everyone else. He sins, argues with his wife, gets discouraged, battles to get time for a quality devotional life, becomes frustrated with his job, gets angry, and needs to share his heart with someone. Yet his position seems to build a wall around him. Leadership isolates him. The pressure to be publically perfect hounds him. Even in his own church he can be a man on the outside looking in.

Why does this isolation exist? There are many reasons—some with real foundations:

- Fear of criticism from members of the congregation if he gets too friendly with a few people
- Bad experiences of sharing deeply with someone who later used it against him
- Teaching in seminary that he should *not* enter into deep exclusive friendship with someone in the congregation
- Resistance of people in the congregation to develop a deepening friendship knowing all the relational pressures the pastor is under
- Fear of developing friendship outside of the established church leadership circle
- Fear of discussing his real job problems with anyone in the congregation
- Feeling that he can relate as a close friend only to other pastors
- Unspoken pressure to be friends with everyone and disapproval of favoritism
- Little sense of need for friends outside his marriage and family.

It is important that the pastor and his wife enjoy healthy friendships, not only to supply their personal needs but also to set a good example for the congregation. If the pastor and his wife wish to develop intimate and close friendships *inside* the congregation, several things are necessary.

- The pastor must make a conscious decision to allow friendships to develop.
- The pastor must actively seek to develop and pray for these friendships.
- He must be open to rebuke, and be willing to risk being misunderstood or criticized.
- He must guard the confidentiality of information obtained in counseling or other activities as any

professional person would.

- He must be willing to invest time.
- He must be open with his board about the friendship. It should not be secretive.
- The friendship should be open enough to include others in a social way.
- He must mentally and emotionally resist the pressure to be close friends with everyone.

In addition to friendships within the congregation, it helps to have one or two intimate friendships outside the church. They may be friendships that carried over from a previous church or someone from another congregation in the same geographical area.

There are serious consequences when a pastor does not develop these kinds of friendships. He becomes isolated from his congregation and from real relationships; his family (wife and children) suffers from lack of normal relationships; he loses a significant emotional outlet and source of encouragement; and he may not have anyone who will warn him of sin or hold him spiritually accountable.

If you would like to befriend your pastor, use the suggestions and principles in chapter four, and look for practical ways that you can lift his load and help and serve his family. As the relationship develops, take special care to guard its confidentiality, and never take advantage of the relationship in church affairs. If your pastor is married, include his wife in the friendship.

Let's recognize the dilemma our pastor faces in being a leader of people. Encourage him to develop normal friendships, and be tolerant when you are not the recipient of his close friendship. After all, he and his wife are people with needs like everyone else. Draw them in as full participants in friendships within the fellowship.

Summary

1. The church faces six major dilemmas in generating friendships:

There is no longer a survival necessity for interdependence within the local church.

True neighborhoods today are either few or none.

The automobile has changed the nature of the church.

The church is a melting pot of people.

Conflicts arise over petty issues.

The church has been weakened as the primary source of spiritual input for Christians today.

2. A church that generates friendships has a strong spiritual outreach as well as a strong ministry to the body.

3. A church can stimulate friendships by following these suggestions:

Develop small groups.

Teach and practice friendship.

Encourage homogeneous functions.

Teach and encourage hospitality.

Teach and practice conflict resolution.

Stimulate biblical fellowship.

Principles

1. Everyone has a *limited* capacity for friendship, and each person has a *different* capacity for numbers of friendships.

2. As Christians, we are obligated to extend to every person unlimited acceptance *but not* unlimited friendship.

3. Social groupings legitimately exist in the church.

4. Problems and conflict will always be present in any church body.

5. Every person has idealistic expectations both for friendship and for church relationships—which will never be perfectly met.

6. Biblical friendships in the church are developed in the midst of spiritual battle.

7. New Christians are drawn into the fellowship by friends.

8. Pastors and their wives need personal friends.

CHAPTER 11

Friendship with Non-Christians

JIM AND KAREN ROBINSON dropped their two children at the church for a Saturday outing with young people. Instead of going home and plunging into the weekend chores, they drove to a coffee shop for breakfast. They were obviously troubled and said very little as they were served. Finally Karen said, "Jim, I just can't understand it. We've known Al and Bonnie for eight years. I was certain they would at least accept our invitation to discuss having a Bible study."

"Me, too. But I'm just as puzzled that the Carsons and the Parks turned me down flat. We've got a big zero!"

"But why, Jim? We've never pushed our Christianity on them. They acted as if we were strangers when we asked them to our home."

"I really don't understand it. We followed the pastor's instructions to the letter. We listed our friends. We prayed for them. We contacted each of them personally and invited them for dessert at our house. We were honest and explained that we wanted to organize a four-week investigative Bible study and asked them to consider it. We promised there would be no pressure and that they could decide after that first get-together if they wanted to join the study. But everyone made excuses—some of them pretty lame ones too."

"You know, I've sensed a coolness in several of the wives over the last two years."

"It makes me wonder, Karen, if they really are our friends anymore. When was the last time we did anything with them socially? Over a year ago, wasn't it?"

Jim and Karen analyzed and wondered for almost an hour. They finally concluded that their friendship with these non-Christian people had died long ago and they had not known it. They went on thinking they were still friends, but did nothing to maintain or build the relationships. A brief look at their history will reveal some of what happened.

Jim was an up-and-coming businessman. He was talented and ambitious. He and Karen were socially active both in his company and in their neighborhood. A week rarely went by when they did not entertain and attend some social function. They were bright spots in the party circle. Karen was active in community affairs, women's concern groups, and the school PTA.

They did not regularly attend church, but went occasionally at Christmas and Easter. They considered themselves religious in a private way. Jim's background was non-religious. Karen came from a church-going Christian family. She made a personal commitment to

Christ as a teenager, but abandoned any type of Christian practice when she was in college.

As time passed, Karen became disturbed at the quickening pace of their lifestyle and the absence of God from any part of it. She and Jim argued more and enjoyed each other less. Finally they decided to start attending church again. After a few months Jim recognized his need of Christ and accepted Christ as his Savior. Karen recommitted her life to Christ at the same time.

Then their entire lives underwent radical changes. Ambitions assumed a biblical perspective. Their marriage strengthened. Their social life in the party world died. They began to focus on spiritual growth, their family, and church activities.

All the change was largely for the best. But what they didn't see was the subtle separation taking place between themselves and longtime friends. They witnessed to them openly. They turned down party invitations. They withdrew from most non-spiritual activities. They wrapped themselves into a Christian cocoon, isolated from meaningful relationships outside it.

At the coffee shop it dawned on them that they had placed themselves in Christian isolation. They had lost their personal influence on the world. They were cheered on by Christians. They shared their testimonies and they studied the Bible. They grew spiritually, but they climbed out of the world and pulled the ladder up after them. Their link with the past broke and their friends no longer listened to them.

A new Christian often virtually isolates himself from his non-Christian friends in about two to three years unless he makes a point of keeping those friendships current. As he loses touch, he loses one of the key means of witness.

How can we prevent this from happening and still keep ourselves from sin? Should we even try to maintain or develop close friendships with non-Christians?

Our Biblical Precedent

Paul tells the Corinthians in his second epistle to them, "Do not be yoked together with unbelievers. For what do righteousness and wickedness have in common? Or what fellowship can light have with darkness? What harmony is there between Christ and Belial? What does a believer have in common with an unbeliever?" (2 Corinthians 6:14-15).

From this verse, an argument could be developed to say that we cannot be friends with non-Christians. From Jewish history and practice we recall that the Jews could not even eat with the Gentiles, much less be friends. In these verses Paul clearly states that on some level there is a real separation between Christians and non-Christians. But before we attempt to understand Paul's distinction, let's put his instructions within the context of Christ's life and ministry.

Fortunately, Jesus Christ himself broke the ancient Jewish pattern of separation and paved the way for a new set of relationships with non-Christians. Jesus was accused of being "a friend of tax collectors and 'sinners' " (Luke 7:34). When he was attacked for eating and drinking with these tax collectors and sinners, he answered, "It is not the healthy who need a doctor, but the sick. I have not come to call the righteous, but sinners to repentance" (Luke 5:31). Jesus set a new pattern in his ministry of relating to the unbeliever. He didn't avoid believers, but his relationships were not exclusively with them.

So then, how do we interpret 2 Corinthians 6:14? Observe the key word: *yoked*, or bound. The word picture is one of mixing in an inseparable fashion. R.H.C. Lenski translated it as "heterogeneously yoked" (*Interpretation of I & II Corinthians*, Oxford Publishing House, 1937). R.V.G. Tasker says of this verse, "(Paul) now insists with great emphasis that no permanent relationships must be formed between Christians and heathen" (*The Second Epistle of Corinthians, An Introduction and Commentary*, Eerdmans, 1958). Permanent, inseparable relationships such as marriage fit this Scripture, not friendship or social interaction.

Jesus intends for us to develop relationships with non-Christians in the normal course of our lives. How else can we be light and salt in our work, neighborhoods, and society? Our relationships must go beyond preaching or telling the gospel once, and then breaking the relationship if there is no response. We must stick with our friends over a period of time to help them see the difference Christ makes in our lives.

Should we be friends with non-Christians? Yes. We are under obligation to search them out and to befriend them as Christ would have done.

But how? That is the great need. Even if we want to befriend them, we often run up against obstacles which keep us from developing close friendships with non-Christians.

Stumbling Blocks

The hindrances are few in number, but great in their effect. Significant differences do exist between Christians and non-Christians. They approach life from different viewpoints. In forming or keeping friendships, key elements of communication may not be there.

A lack of common spiritual experience and dimension hinders totally open communication. The issue arises out of Paul's instructions in 2 Corinthians 6:14–15, which we've already examined. Although we saw that this passage does permit a friendship, it also establishes the lack of specific spiritual ground for such a relationship. We can not easily share what really grips our hearts and minds in our walk with Christ. As we interact with non-Christians we may find that the most important issues of our lives are not the same.

We may engage in different lifestyles and interest patterns. A high percentage of many Christians' optional activities involve meetings with the church and relationships with other Christians. Although we need to grow through fellowship, we must guard against creating different worlds which never touch each other. Christians and non-Christians simply do not engage in enough overlapping areas of activities.

Christians and non-Christians are not always naturally attracted to one another. Their lifestyle may turn us off. Or ours may turn them off. Even conversation can dry up if we've allowed ourselves to grow out of touch with concerns outside of Christian circles. Unless we seek out and maintain friendships with non-Christians, it is too easy for us to slide into the dangerous attitude of complacency. "I'll get along with you if I have to, but don't encroach on my personal space," we seem to say.

Our motives for developing a friendship are too often evangelistic in nature. Non-Christians see through these motives. A conditional, recruiting friendship rarely lives long. Who wants to be a notch on a spiritual gun? But what can we do about this? How can we be a true friend without sharing Jesus Christ, the most important part of our lives?

We can't. But we can clarify and improve our motives. And we can get over the hurdles that separate us from non-Christian friends.

Making Friends with Non-Christians

Friendships with non-Christians keep us in touch with "reality." The majority of the world is non-Christian. The reclusive life in a Christian environment is unknown to most unbelievers, and they need special sight to see the ultimate reality of the Christian life. Non-Christians need a keyhole to look through. Perhaps your life and friendship could be that special keyhole.

Clarify your motives. Christians are often caught in a dilemma: We can never pursue a meaningful friendship with a non-Christian without envisioning their coming to Christ, yet as we mentioned above, evangelistic motives can be a stumbling block to that same meaningful friendship. Clarifying our motives may help to resolve this dilemma.

We must distinguish between evangelism *in the course of* friendship and friendship *for the purpose of* evangelism. We cannot deny our inner drive and disobey Christ's specific command to evangelize. In some sense it is part of any relationship with non-Christians, and our life in Christ must affect that relationship. We cannot suppress who and what we are.

Our motive in developing a friendship with a non-Christian, however, *includes* evangelism, but it should not be *only* for evangelism. We love our friends for many reasons. As we love them, we demonstrate it by sharing the most significant issue of our lives—Jesus Christ. In a true friendship, they will respect that which means so much to us.

The problem arises when the friendship is motivated *only* by evangelism, and our friends sense it. They feel manipulated. Friendship only for evangelism is not wrong, but it does have risks. We prefer to call that *relationships* for evangelism. Friendship may naturally develop within the context of such relationships, but evangelism is the focus.

In his fine book, *Life-Style Evangelism* (Multnomah Press, 1981), Dr. Joseph C. Aldrich says, "Witness begins with *presence*, moves to *proclamation*, and then on to *persuasion*" (page 202). He describes presence as the flavor or music of our lives which attracts others to God. Proclamation is the direct presentation of the gospel message. Persuasion is the encouragement to make a final decision to become a Christian.

Jim Peterson, in his book *Evangelism as a Lifestyle* (Navpress, 1980), emphasizes that we must be willing to emerge from our Christian isolation and enter the arena where the non-Christian lives.

> Such isolation has a destructive effect on a local body of Christians, as well as destroying our communication with the lost. Christians who keep to themselves, who do not experience a continuing influx of people just arriving from the dominion of darkness, soon surround themselves with their own subculture. Receiving no feedback from people fresh from the world, they forget what it's like out there. Peculiar language codes, behavioral patterns, and communication techniques emerge that only have meaning for insiders. As such, a local body becomes increasingly ingrown. Eventually, communication with the man on the street is impossible. (page 88)

As we relate outwardly to the lost, we must do so not just out of obligation, but out of real love for others. God will honor that motive for friendship. Non-Christians will read and accept that motive without suspicion.

Decide to do it. We believe that expanding your

friendship circle to include non-Christians requires a definite decision. It does not just happen. Just as it takes conscious effort to develop a Christian friendship, so it also takes a conscious decision and effort to pursue a non-Christian friendship. It may mean joining activities where you will find non-Christians.

Find friends in the ordinary course of life and work. Imagine yourself walking down a busy sidewalk. A stranger stops you and asks, "Pardon me, but would you consider being my friend?" Your mind runs through a series of replies from "Why?" to "Don't bother me." You no doubt think, "What an odd way to get a friend." That is no way to find a friend, Christian or non-Christian.

God placed you in a unique set of circumstances in which you can find many sources of non-Christian relationships. Think of these natural settings. The past may include high school and college, your old neighborhood, family—aunts, uncles, cousins—and former jobs. Perhaps your present circumstances include neighbors, co-workers and professional colleagues, club members, relatives and in-laws, parents of your children's friends, or school functions. Future situations might bring new neighbors, extended family through your children's marriages, and new co-workers.

Don't let old friendships die. They are irreplaceable. We have seen several of those casual friendships of fifteen and twenty years in the past redevelop as paths cross and needs change. Most still remain at the casual level. Some are individual with one of us and some friendships involve us as a couple. Keep some of those people on your Christmas card list and see if you can renew friendships.

Over the years I have made a concerted effort to maintain contact with many relationships of the past. I regularly call and see my fifth grade teacher and my high school history teacher. For several years I have pursued a particular high school acquaintance who experienced great public popularity, then fell into obscurity. I used to visit one childhood friend regularly when he was in prison. I looked him up several times in later years. Anyone can make friendship overtures to acquaintances from the past.—(Jerry)

Be where non-Christian friendships can develop. Although we make initial contacts at work or across the fence, seldom do the friendships develop there. They need a more sociable environment. In their home or yours, at a sports event or party, in a community club or on a fishing trip—*be there.* Your presence opens doors. Have you noticed how different the conversation will be at a company picnic compared to the office or shop? The relaxed atmosphere puts people at ease and produces a good climate for friendship.

In my years in the Air Force, I deliberately entered activities in which I could enjoy social interaction with non-Christians. I frequently played on fast-pitch softball teams. I played with and coached an Air Force Academy faculty volleyball team. I played handball with other faculty members. I joined the chess club for a year. We made department socials a priority. We felt that these activities were a key to our non-Christian friendships.—(Jerry)

Don't hide your Christianity. Fly your flag early. This does not mean a verbal witness the first time you are introduced. But as you talk, the fact that you attend church, read your Bible, or have religious beliefs should emerge naturally over a period of time.

Share how your daughter came home from Sunday school telling of some humorous incident. Mention that your son asked a tough Bible question that took you an hour to find the answer. Share things "in passing," not as a crowbar for opening the door to deep conversation. Be honest, but not pushy. Your religious beliefs should not be a deep dark secret in a developing friendship.

A fellow faculty member at the Air Force Academy and I had known each other since 1962. In the first months of our acquaintance he asked some advice on teaching Sunday school at the base chapel, although he was not a Christian. This led to occasional religious discussions over the next eight years. In 1975 he called and asked to see me. He was deeply troubled over an incident with his son and wanted prayer. A few days later he received Christ. Thirteen years of casual friendship were part of God's plan of reaching him. But if my Christianity had been hidden, he never would have asked the initial question in 1962.—(Jerry)

Look for common interests or goals. A friendship often grows around something like a pearl grows around a grain of sand. Sports, children, schools, professional development, sewing, gardening, politics—each of these could be a starting point. If you have to, broaden your interests. Observe what people enjoy and ask them about it. Talk about what you enjoy. When you strike that common chord, you will both know it.

Make friends with people you like. Here again we are discussing friendship, not just evangelism. Ask God to develop in you a love for people. Display your interest in them and be a magnet to draw them to God. We all find ourselves drawn to certain people for various reasons. Use that attraction as a basis for friendship.

Use your home. Your home reveals who you are more than any other environment. Bring people into that part of your life. They will see your books, your children, the kind of furniture you like, your hobbies, your tastes, and your relationships. They'll absorb all of this information and decide whether or not they like you or want to pursue a friendship with you. And you may receive an invitation to their home, which will help you make the same decisions.

Pray for keys to friendship. A friendship seldom develops around every aspect of our lives; usually two or three common interests bring us together and generate topics of conversation. Pray that you will observe these keys and be able to pursue them. Ask God to make you sensitive to others' interests and needs, and pray that they will be responsive to your overtures of friendship. And of course, ask God to make Christ evident to them through your life.

Look for special needs. At certain times of life people are more eager for friends than at others—when they are new to a city or job, when a divorce occurs, when a teenager gets into trouble, when the job begins to disintegrate, or when illness strikes. If we remain alert, our opportunity to develop the friendship may come through that specific need.

Another casual friend with whom I worked for two years beginning in 1962 called me again in 1977, thirteen years after our last communication. His marriage had dissolved and he was troubled and sought both help and friendship. Four years later he received Christ through contact with several Christians—almost nineteen years after our first contact.—(Jerry)

Be patient—don't force the friendship. A certain

tentativeness characterizes the initial stages of a friendship. If things move too fast, the friendship can be smothered and snuffed out. Remember that everyone has other friendships and relationships that must be maintained. They will not abandon everything to pursue a friendship with you. Plan on taking a year to develop the friendship at a casual pace; this allows plenty of time and space for healthy communication. Ask God for wisdom in how quickly or slowly to pursue the friendship.

Accept them as they are. Don't try to change new friends. You want them to accept you as you are—a religious person. You need to communicate the same acceptance to them, regardless of what they do. Keep in mind Thoreau's remark, "The most I can do for my friend is simply to be his friend" (*Journal*, February 7, 1841).

How to be Attractive to Others

The mystery of human attraction continues to puzzle scientists and psychologists. The magnetism between two distinct personalities defies description both in romance and in friendship. All the computer analysis in the world will never solve the matching chemistry between two human personalities, because the most unusual friendship can develop in spite of disparities in personality and interests. Yet certain characteristics do play a significant part in *initial* attraction, particularly between believers and unbelievers.

Have you ever noticed how some people possess a charisma that draws people to them? Some people have it and some don't. But as you go beyond the issues of personality, some common threads of attraction begin to emerge.

Inevitably, material success and social status stimulate initial attraction, if for no other reason than vicarious fascination. But if these are not backed up by an attractive *person* underneath, the attraction will quickly fade. These factors can be useful only in whetting someone's interest. The quality of an individual life is what really counts.

Most of us have little control over success and status factors anyway. We *can* focus on becoming more attractive to non-Christians, however, no matter what our position in life, by striving to develop the following characteristics.

Christlikeness. "When they saw the courage of Peter and John and realized that they were unschooled, ordinary men, they were astonished and they took note that these men had been with Jesus" (Acts 4:13). We become like the person we spend the most time with. As we spend time with Jesus, we become like him, and people sense it. All our efforts to attract others are worthless if Jesus Christ is not honored in the process. The aroma of Christ in us attracts people in a way that surpasses all others.

This subject, which could really be a separate book, underlies all other issues. But to be Christlike we must do those things which build Christlikeness—a personal devotional life, obedience to his word, study of his word, and fellowship with other Christians. Do people see a difference in your life? Do they observe you and take note that you have been with Jesus? This is the master magnet of a truly attractive life. Build it at all costs.

Godly response to suffering. No one wants to suffer, yet most of us will suffer physically or emotionally in some way in the next few years. What response will characterize your life then? Bitterness? Complaints? Despair? Joy? Patience? Whatever your response, people will notice it. They often watch with morbid fascination as another person struggles through the deeper problems of life. The spectacle of suffering is a magnet.

If you respond in a godly way to your sufferings and trials, non-Christians will take note and privately wonder why. Then, as they face personal suffering, they may turn to you as a source of help. Perhaps even without a problem of their own, they may ask why your response was different. As you struggle in your suffering, remember that your life is being transformed into a magnet that draws people to you and to God. Let God use you in a special way in times of distress.

Honesty. In a world where honesty and ethics often take a back seat to expediency and opportunity, a truly honest person stands out above the crowd. The way we speak, work, or do business makes a definite impression on people. As people grapple with issues of ethics in their work, others watch how they respond, fully expecting them to opt for their own selfish interests when opportunity exists. A Christian who refuses to lie, stretch the truth, or falsify a document certainly attracts notice. Though some will be turned off by honesty, because they don't want to face their own guilt, others will be drawn to it in respect and admiration.

Generosity. People love a generous person. One who truly gives time, money, or help will always attract friends. Adopt a Christlike, giving spirit and you will be rewarded with the pleasure of helping others as well as with the satisfaction of drawing others to you.

Competence. Not everyone will succeed spectacularly, but everyone *can* achieve a measure of success by performing competently at his respective level of ability. A successful person always wields an influence in some circle of people, whether that person is a wife with a knack for decorating, a mechanic who can fix anything, an engineer who can see through problems, a student who gets high grades, a salesman who excells in selling, or a dependable and responsible manager. As we develop competence in our tasks at work, in the home, or even in our hobbies, we attract people who come to us out of respect, for our instruction and help.

No matter what you do, if you dedicate it to the Lord and perform it to the best of your ability, your life will attract others.

A strong marriage. As marriages crumble around us, the stable, happy marriage shines like a spotlight on a black night. As non-Christians struggle in their marriages, they grope for answers but rarely know where to turn. Our society's confusion on the family clouds the issue even more. A truly happy couple appears unique.

Is your marriage attractive? Can people see contrasts to the world's standards in your marriage? They should. If they do, you will attract even non-Christians and open the door to a friendship. Others long to know the secret to a happy marriage. Share your secret with them.

Close and loving family bonds. Ask parents in their forties about their children and you will probably strike a sensitive area. Few people, Christian or non-Christian, escape the hazards and hassles of raising teenagers. If your family grapples successfully with the issues of raising children in both younger and teen years, you will have a significant platform for attracting others.

Results speak louder than sermons. As you talk with non-Christians, the issue of children will probably open lines of communication. But telling is insufficient. People need to see and relate to your family. Invite them to your home and let them observe you firsthand. No family is perfect, but if you have tried to apply biblical principles in raising your children, chances are they will notice a difference in your home. Allow your family to attract non-Christians.

We can and should build friendships with non-Christians. We must guard against becoming hermit Christians, and instead respond to the great need and opportunity to be Christ's man or woman in the midst of a secular world. May God grant us the heart and vision to befriend the lost of the world, and to befriend each other as we draw closer to him.

Summary

1. We can and should develop friendships with non-Christians. Christ himself set the example.

2. Some of the things that may get in the way of our developing friendships with non-Christians are:
   lack of common spiritual dimension, different lifestyles and interests, lack of natural attraction, and evangelistic motives for friendship.

3. Use the following suggestions to make friends with non-Christians:
   Clarify your motives.
   Decide to do it.
   Find friends in the course of daily life.
   Be where non-Christian friendships can develop.
   Don't hide your Christianity.
   Look for common interests.
   Make friends with people you like.
   Use your home.
   Pray for keys to friendship.
   Look for special needs.
   Be patient—don't force the friendship.
   Accept them as they are.

4. We can make ourselves more attractive to others by cultivating these qualities:

Christlikeness, godly response to suffering, honesty, generosity, competence, strong marriage, and close and loving family bonds.

Evaluating Your Friendship Potential

Self-Evaluation Inventory

When you want to drive to a certain city, you first must establish where you are before you can determine how you're going to get to your destination. As you seek to improve your friendship–making ability and depth, you need to know something of what you are like now as a friend and what you should work on to improve your ability to make and keep friends. This self-evaluation inventory will help you discover where your personal strengths and weaknesses lie.

As you answer the questions on the following pages, be as honest and realistic with yourself as you can. Don't search for the "right" answers, but for those that most accurately fit you and your personal experience.

Instructions: Circle the *one* answer that most fits what you do in your relationships *now*. Though you will occasionally want to supply more than one answer, choose only one. Some of the questions are meant to be ambiguous in order to get you thinking creatively about yourself.

1. When you hear someone gossiping about your friend, you
   a. get angry inside.
   b. keep silent.
   c. defend your friend.
   d. confront that person for gossiping.

2. The friends you see regularly share deep feelings with you
   a. frequently.
   b. never.
   c. occasionally.
   d. Only one or two of them share their deep feelings with you.

3. In your closest friendship, you
   a. goof around and have fun most of the time.
   b. rarely laugh, since you focus on serious topics.
   c. enjoy being together, but are often emotionally exhausted afterward.
   d. frequently laugh or have fun times mixed with serious.

4. You are attracted to people who
   a. make you think.
   b. ask lots of questions.
   c. keep controversial opinions to themselves.
   d. tend to agree with you most of the time.

5. As a friend you
   a. often encourage others.
   b. have a difficult time encouraging others, but really want to.
   c. seldom seem to encourage others.
   d. feel your role is more as a confronter than an encourager.

6. In the past three months, you
   a. helped a friend at significant cost.
   b. have not helped a friend at any cost to yourself.
   c. helped when it was inconvenient to you.
   d. significantly changed your plans to help.

7. Have you ever expressed to a friend that you love and appreciate him or her?
   a. Yes.
   b. No.
   c. Not in those terms, but you have said that you value his or her friendship.
   d. No, but you have wanted to do so.

8. Tonight you are going to a concert you've been looking forward to for several weeks. An hour before leaving you receive a call from one of your better friends. His car stalled twenty-five miles away and he needs a ride home. Your response is to
   a. get upset inside, but help anyway.
   b. tell him you can't help.
   c. tell him of your plans, but offer to come by.
   d. tell him you will make arrangements for help or be there yourself.

9. You pray with your friends
   a. only when one of you has an urgent request.
   b. as often as you meet.
   c. never.
   d. occasionally.

10. How many friends do you have now that have been friends since high school or college?
    a. None.
    b. 1-2.
    c. 3-4.
    d. 5 or more.

11. As a friend, you
    a. draw others strongly to a deeper spiritual walk.
    b. have some influence on others to live a more spiritual life.
    c. have little influence on others to live a more spiritual life.

12. You help your friends
    a. in practical ways whenever they ask.
    b. very little in practical ways.
    c. by looking for ways to serve them, instead of waiting until they ask.
    d. occasionally, but often feel you are intruding.

13. When you interact with your friends, you
    a. do not like to be confronted.
    b. want them to confront you whenever they see a need in your life.
    c. want their input only when you ask.

14. When a friend shares a serious personal problem with you, you
    a. never tell another person.
    b. occasionally share it in confidence with another.
    c. frequently tell others.
    d. tell only a person who you feel could help.

15. When talking with a friend, you
    a. interrupt often.
    b. seldom interrupt.
    c. remember little of what was said.
    d. never interrupt or even question.

16. In your time with friends, you enjoy
    a. keeping the focus on spiritual things.
    b. doing something you both have an interest in.
    c. participating in group activities more than doing things together.

17. As a person you are
    a. boring to be with.
    b. able to stimulate other people's thinking without angering them.
    c. stimulating, but often get an angry response.
    d. one who has lots of ideas but rarely shares them.

18. When you seek a friendship, you consider spiritual interaction
    a. a major issue.
    b. a concern only after the friendship is well underway.
    c. a minor issue.
    d. very important, since you must have doctrinal agreement to maintain friendship.

19. You encourage your friends in their personal spiritual devotions
    a. frequently.
    b. occasionally.
    c. rarely.
    d. never, since you don't even discuss spiritual issues.

20. When you talk to your friends, you
    a. reveal your thoughts openly, not attemping to guard your words.
    b. speak very carefully, making sure you say the right thing.
    c. often speak harshly, then feel you need to apologize.
    d. speak freely, as long as you can be both kind and honest.

21. In the past, you have broken a confidence from a friend
    a. frequently.
    b. rarely.
    c. never.

22. In the past year, you have told some of your deepest thoughts and struggles
    a. to a friend (not your spouse).
    b. to your pastor or a counselor.
    c. to no one, even though you wanted to.
    d. to no one, because you did not desire to share them with anyone.

23. Consider two or three of your closest friends. In the last two months,
    a. at least one has discussed with you some aspect of your personal spiritual life.
    b. none of them has discussed any spiritual topic with you that is personal.
    c. at least one has discussed a spiritual topic, but not on a personal level.
    d. none of them has discussed any spiritual issue with you.

24. As a listener you rate yourself as
    a. very good, giving the impression both of hearing and of understanding.
    b. good, on only a few occasions showing impatience.
    c. moderate, not always consistent in your attention.
    d. poor, often impatient or unconcerned.

25. When you do not approve of what a friend says or does,
    a. you immediately confront him.
    b. you indicate disapproval by facial expression or tone of voice.
    c. you never say what you think, but ask questions about his actions or words.
    d. you share what you think, but only when he asks, or at a later time.

26. People who are just casual friends of yours
    a. rarely share their feelings with you.
    b. often seek you out when they are troubled.

c. sometimes tell you what they're really feeling, but only if you draw it out of them.

d. give you the "silent treatment" when they are feeling bad.

27. When talking to a close friend, you
   a. find it difficult to say what you really think.
   b. find it easy to say what you really think.
   c. want to say what you really think, but seldom do.

d. guard your words carefully so you don't reveal your feelings.

28. In your relationships with your closest friends, you
   a. don't touch them physically, except for a handshake.
   b. occasionally give them a warm embrace.
   c. usually touch them physically in some way (take an arm, hand or shoulder) beyond a handshake.

Scoring

Transfer your answers from the inventory to the Score Sheet on pages 189 to 190.

1. Circle the number under the corresponding letter you chose for each question. For instance, if you chose answer "b" for question 4, you would circle the "2" on the score sheet.

2. Total all the numbers circled and enter in the "Total Score" blank.

3. Each question relates to a specific area of friendship as shown by the words in this key. Total up the points for each area and put this total in the corresponding blank under "Specific Area Scores." For instance, if your scores for questions 1, 10, 14 and 21 were 5, 3, 3, and 5 respectively, you would enter the number 16 in the blank under "Loyalty." You scored 16 out of a possible 20 points in that area.

SCORE SHEET

Circle the number under your response.

	a.	b.	c.	d.	
1.	2	1	5	2	Loyalty
2.	5	0	2	4	Sharing
3.	1	1	3	5	Fun
4.	5	2	0	1	Stimulation
5.	5	3	0	1	Encouragement
6.	5	0	3	4	Self-Sacrifice
7.	5	0	3	2	Love
8.	3	0	2	5	Self-Sacrifice
9.	1	5	0	4	Spiritual Challenge
10.	0	3	4	5	Loyalty
11.	5	3	0	-	Spiritual Challenge
12.	3	0	5	2	Encouragement
13.	0	5	3	-	Stimulation
14.	3	2	0	5	Loyalty
15.	2	5	1	0	Sharing
16.	1	5	3	-	Fun
17.	1	5	1	3	Stimulation
18.	5	2	0	1	Spiritual Challenge
19.	5	4	2	0	Spiritual Challenge
20.	1	3	3	5	Sharing
21.	0	5	3	-	Loyalty
22.	5	3	2	0	Sharing
23.	5	2	2	0	Spiritual Challenge
24.	5	4	2	0	Sharing
25.	3	2	1	5	Sharing
26.	1	5	2	0	Sharing
27.	1	5	3	1	Sharing
28.	0	5	4	-	Love

TOTAL SCORE _____

Out of possible 140

Specific Area Scores

1. Loyalty   (1, 10, 14, 21) _____ out of 20

2. Sharing   (2, 15, 20, 22, 24, 25, 26, 27) _____ out of 40

3. Fun   (3, 16) _____ out of 10

4. Stimulation   (4, 13, 17) _____ out of 15

5. Encouragement   (5, 12) _____ out of 10

6. Self-Sacrifice   (6, 8) _____ out of 10

7. Love   (7, 28) _____ out of 10

8. Spiritual Challenge   (9, 11, 18, 19, 23) _____ out of 25

Evaluating Your Score

Now that you have scored yourself, compare your score to the scale below. Remember that no test is perfect, and this scoring has a great deal of latitude. It serves as an *indicator* of your friendship potential and needs. The highest score possible is 140.

125 to 140   You are so friendly you will replace Rover as man's best friend. Excellent friendship potential.

110 to 124   You have very good potential to develop deep and well-rounded friendships.

95 to 109   You have good potential for developing friendships, but could work on a few specific areas.

85 to 94   You probably have a small number of deeper friends and could develop them further by working on some specific areas.

Below 85   You are most likely a lonely person with significant needs for friendship development.

Remember that this information is a guide for development. Now that you have a general indication of your friendship potential, take a look at your Specific Area Scores. Each question in the inventory is keyed to one of the characteristics in chapter one.

1. Check to see if there were any areas where you scored very low (such as loyalty).
2. Examine carefully those questions where you scored 0 to 2. Use chapter one to help you develop these areas.
3. Write out two or three specific areas in which you need or would like help. Keep them in mind and review chapters one and five, then write out some initial steps you can take to start improving.

If you scored quite low, doublecheck your addition and then review your answers. You might also want to have a close friend or your spouse take the test as if he or she were you. You may have scored yourself unrealistically high or low if you lack good self-perception.

As you seek to apply the principles of this book, keep the areas of need in mind and work specifically on them. Your friendship potential depends only on your willingness to learn, grow, and reach out to others.